IMAGES OF

UNITED STATES INFANTRY WEAPONS OF THE SECOND WORLD WAR

RARE PHOTOGRAPHS FROM WARTIME ARCHIVES

Michael Green

Pen & Sword
MILITARY

First published in Great Britain in 2015 by
PEN & SWORD MILITARY
An imprint of
Pen & Sword Books Ltd
47 Church Street
Barnsley
South Yorkshire
S70 2AS

ISBN 978-1-47382-722-6

Typeset by Concept, Huddersfield, West Yorkshire HD4 5JL.
Printed and bound in India by Replika Press Pvt. Ltd.

Pen & Sword Books Ltd incorporates the imprints of Pen & Sword Archaeology, Atlas, Aviation, Battleground, Discovery, Family History, History, Maritime, Military, Naval, Politics, Railways, Select, Social History, Transport, True Crime, and Claymore Press, Frontline Books, Leo Cooper, Praetorian Press, Remember When, Seaforth Publishing and Wharncliffe.

For a complete list of Pen & Sword titles please contact
PEN & SWORD BOOKS LIMITED
47 Church Street, Barnsley, South Yorkshire, S70 2AS, England
E-mail: enquiries@pen-and-sword.co.uk
Website: www.pen-and-sword.co.uk

Contents

Dedication

I would like to dedicate this book to Alan Cors,
founder and Chairman of the American in Wartime Museum,
for his help and support over these many years.

Acknowledgments

As with any published work, authors must depend on their friends for assistance. For this work, they include Michael Panchyshyn and Martin Morgan. The bulk of the historical photographs in this work were acquired from the National Archives. In addition, Gunnery Sergeant (Ret.) Thomas E. Williams (former director of the United States Marine Corps Historical Company) provided contemporary images of Marine Corps Second World War re-enactors armed with historical weapons.

For brevity's sake, pictures credited to the National Archives will be shortened to 'NA' and those from the United States Marine Corps Historical Company are shortened to 'USMCHC'.

Introduction

During the Second World War, American soldiers and Marines experienced combat in a variety of challenging environments, against a number of different foes. Despite the worldwide conflict often being defined by the actions of large numbers of aircraft and warships, there continued to be a tactical landscape in which hand-held infantry weapons mattered as much they ever had. On many occasions, it would be American infantrymen firing from hastily dug foxholes, refusing to give in to fierce enemy onslaughts that swayed the course of battles.

It was during this time in history that the rifles, pistols, carbines, and submachine guns used by soldiers and marines earned a special reputation for ruggedness and effectiveness that proved Americans were among the world's best weapon makers. Some of the best known of these small arms were the legendary M1911 pistol, the incomparable semi-automatic M1 Garand, the unstoppable Browning Automatic Rifle (BAR), and the Thompson submachine gun, which also saw service with the British Army during the Second World War. There were also a few failures, such as the Johnson Rifle and the Reising submachine gun.

American hand-held infantry small arms were supported in combat by a number of infantry crew-served weapons, such as machine guns, antitank rocket launchers, mortars, recoilless rifles, and flamethrowers. The best known of these crew-served infantry support weapons were the .30 and .50 caliber machine guns, both water-cooled and air-cooled, designed by famous American inventor John M. Browning. The latter, in its air-cooled version, continues to serve with the American military today.

On the larger end of the spectrum of infantry support weapons employed by American soldiers and Marines during the Second World War, there were some towed weapons. These encompassed both the 37mm and 57mm antitank guns, the latter a British-derived weapon. In addition, there was the short-range 75mm Pack M1A1 and the 105mm M2A1 and M3 howitzers, which offered fire-support in an indirect role to the mortars of the infantry units of both the U.S. Army and U.S. Marine Corps. In addition, tanks were a divisional asset of U.S. Marine Corps infantry divisions of the Second World War, but not of U.S. Army infantry divisions until after the Second World War.

Notes to the Reader

During the Second World War, the U.S. Army mobilized ninety-one divisions, of which two were later deactivated. Of the remaining eighty-nine divisions, sixty-six were infantry, with a personnel strength of 15,514 men in the August 1942 Table of Organization and Equipment (TO&E). This figure dropped to approximately 14,037 men in a January 1945 TO&E. If all the U.S. Army non-divisional units of infantry and artillery had been gathered together during the Second World War, six additional infantry divisions could have been formed.

The bulk of the fighting strength of each U.S. Army infantry division was contained within three infantry regiments that totaled from a high in a June 1941 TO&E of 10,020 infantrymen, to a low of 9,204 infantrymen in a January 1945 TO&E. Each U.S. Army infantry regiment consisted of three infantry battalions, which were broken down into three infantry companies per infantry battalion. In turn, each infantry battalion had three rifle companies divided into three infantry platoons. Each infantry platoon was further subdivided into three infantry squads.

The U.S. Marine Corps mobilized six divisions during the Second World War, all of which could be considered infantry divisions. Marine divisions, unlike U.S. Army divisions, were all-arms units, meaning the tanks, artillery, and antiaircraft guns were all organic to the divisional TO&E at different times, including aviation, which will not be covered in this work.

Like the U.S. Army infantry divisions, the six all-arms U.S. Marine Corps divisions went through a number of changes in their TO&E from the divisional level down to the infantry squad level during the Second World War. The U.S. Marine Corps wartime infantry divisions were based on the same triangular organization structure as were U.S. Army Infantry Divisions.

Chapter One

Individual Infantry Weapons

The most widely used handgun in American military (i.e. the U.S. Army and U.S. Marine Corps) service during the Second World War was officially referred to as the Pistol, Automatic, Caliber .45 Model 1911A1. Most referred to it as the '.45', the '.45 automatic', or the 'Colt .45'. It entered into production in 1926 and was an improved version of the original (or first generation) model of the weapon designated the Pistol, Automatic, Caliber Model 1911, employed during the First World War. As so many of the M1911s remained in the inventory, only a small number of the improved second generation A1 variant were built prior to the Second World War.

With America's entry into the Second World War, following the Japanese attack on Pearl Harbor, Hawaii, and with the American military dramatically growing in size, the Colt Patent Firearms Company was contracted to build a large number of the M1911A1 version of the weapon. Because Colt could not construct the quantity asked for by the U.S. Army Ordnance Department (hereafter referred to as merely the Ordnance Department), four civilian firms were contracted by the Ordnance Department to build the weapon. The American military saw the M1911A1 primarily as a defensive weapon and sought to restrict its issue to officers, to some crew-served weapons, and rear area service troops.

A comparison between the M1911A1 and the various German military semi-automatic pistols comes from a U.S. Army report published in March 1945: 'The

---

U.S. Army Ordnance Department

The Ordnance Department was responsible for the design, procurement, distribution, and maintenance of all the U.S. Army's weapons, and by default, the majority of weapons for the U.S. Marine Corps; although, prior to the Second World War, the U.S. Navy, which oversaw the U.S. Marine Corps, acquired some weapons that had not been adopted by the U.S. Army. When a new weapon passed all its acceptance tests it was standardized (accepted/adopted) by the Ordnance Department and ordered into full-scale production. The letter 'M' in a weapon's designation indicated that it had been standardized.

---

standard caliber .45 U.S. automatic is preferred to any of the German-issue pistols. The greater striking power is desired over the advantage of a lightweight weapon. The safety features are considered superior to those of German pistols.'

The only other handgun to see service in any substantial way with the American military during the Second World War was .45 caliber Model 1917 double-action revolver. It was a leftover from the First World War and had been built by both Smith and Wesson and Colt during that conflict. Approximately 15,000 were pulled from storage in 1941 and refurbished before being reissued.

Bolt-Action Rifles

Another First World War era weapon that was updated for use during the Second World War was officially labeled the Rifle, Caliber .30, M1903. The bolt-action rifle had been developed prior to the First World War and was built by both the government-owned Springfield Armory and Rock Island Arsenal. The bolt-action system of operation for the weapon was a derivative of the German military Mauser rifle design.

The Rifle, Caliber .30, M1903 fired the M1906 cartridge commonly referred to as the .30-06 cartridge, which proved to be the standard American rifle and machine gun cartridge of both the First and Second World Wars. The rifle itself was best known to American infantrymen as the 'Springfield 03' or just the '03' and earned a sterling reputation in both war and peacetime for its reliability and accuracy.

The post First World War replacement for the bolt-action M1903 was a semi-automatic rifle that began entering service with the U.S. Army in 1937, but initially in very small numbers. With the lead up to America's official entry into the Second World War the Ordnance Department was forced to resume production of the bolt-action M1903 until production of the new semi-automatic rifle could be ramped up to sufficient levels to meet all its needs.

As the original government-owned facilities that had built the M1903 were busy with other projects prior to America's official entry into the Second World War, the Ordnance Department contracted with the Remington Arms Company to begin production of an identical copy of the First World War era M1903. To speed up the number of rifles built by Remington, the Ordnance Department, together with engineers from the firm, simplified the weapon design, resulting in a new model designated the Rifle, Caliber .30, M1903 (Modified).

Not long after the M1903 (Modified) came about, Remington engineers made some additional modifications to the weapon's design to further speed up the production of the rifle. This resulted in the final version of the weapon designated the Rifle, Caliber .30, Model M1903A3.

To increase the number of M1903A3 rifles being built, the Ordnance Department contracted with the Smith-Corona Typewriter Company to build the weapon.

Production of the M1903A3 was canceled in early 1944 by the Ordnance Department as a sufficient number of the new semi-automatic rifles were now in service.

M1903 Sniper Rifles

There was a dedicated sniper version of the M1903A3 labeled the Rifle, Caliber .30, M1903A4 (Sniper's). The U.S. Army's table of organization (TO&E), during the Second World War, called for one sniper rifle per platoon, although their popularity sometimes found them at the squad level, as seen in this passage from a U.S. Army publication labeled *Combat Lessons No. 5*: 'We had one Springfield 03 Sniper's rifle with scope with each squad. It is absolutely accurate. All the fellows want one. It is not too bulky and can be carried just as easily with as without scope.'

Not happy with the Rifle, Caliber .30, M1903A4 (Sniper's), the U.S. Marine Corps modified some of its pre-Second World War M1903A1 rifles into makeshift sniper rifles during the conflict. The M1903A1 had been standardized in 1926 and differed from the M1903, as it had a pistol grip type stock. The M1903A1s would be fitted with scopes designed and built by the civilian firm of the John Unertl Company and issued in 1942 and 1943.

Pulled from Storage

In addition to the various models of the M1903 brought back into service during the Second World War, the Ordnance Department reached back into its storage warehouses before America's official entry into the conflict and pulled out another First World War era bolt-action rifle labeled the Rifle, Caliber .30, Model of 1917 (Enfield). It was an American-built copy of the British designed and built bolt-action rifle designated as the Short Magazine Lee-Enfield Rifle No. 1, Mark III.

The American model of the Enfield differed from the British Army model, as it fired a .30-06 cartridge rather than the British Army .303 cartridge. Other than a brief appearance with U.S. Army units fighting in North Africa in November 1942, the American version of the Enfield was reserved strictly for stateside training duties and was often the first weapon American soldiers trained on during the early years of the conflict.

Semi-Automatic Rifles

The eventual replacement for the M1903 rifle for the U.S. Army was the Rifle, Caliber .30, M1, a semi-automatic weapon that had originally been contracted for by the Ordnance Department in January 1936, with the first small run of pre-production test examples leaving the Springfield Armory assembly line early the following year.

The first production units of the Rifle, Caliber .30, M1 came out of the Springfield Armory in late 1937, but were built only in small numbers up through 1939, due to production bottlenecks. The Ordnance Department therefore turned to civilian industry and called for bids in the summer of 1939 to build the weapon. Winchester submitted the lowest bid and won the contract.

The Rifle, Caliber .30, M1 was most commonly referred to as the 'M1 rifle' in documents or just 'M1'. Today it is more commonly referred to as the 'Garand', after its designer, John C. Garand, who was the chief civilian Ordnance Department engineer at the Springfield Armory. U.S. Army General George S. Patton called the M1 rifle: 'the greatest battle implement ever devised'.

There had been some minor problems with the early production M1 rifles, which the Ordnance Department considered normal in the development of any new weapon. Unfortunately, these problems attracted the attention of the National Rifle Association (NRA) and the United States Congress, who almost had the production contracts for the rifle canceled in the early part of 1940 over the weapon's perceived shortcomings.

The squabble over the M1 rifle's performance would not end until late 1940, when the U.S. Marine Corps decided to conduct a series of tests to compare the M1 rifle to competing semi-automatic rifles. The M1 rifle proved superior to the other semi-automatic rifles submitted, and was adopted by the U.S. Marine Corps in late 1941. This decision effectively ended the NRA and Congressional criticism of the weapon.

Due to the late adoption of the M1 rifle by the U.S. Marine Corps, when the American military invaded the Japanese-occupied island of Guadalcanal in August 1942, the Marines involved in the operation were still armed with the M1903 bolt-action rifle, whereas the U.S. Army soldiers who took part in the invasion had been equipped with the semi-automatic M1 rifle.

The marines were very impressed with the M1 rifle in the hands of the soldiers fighting on Guadalcanal, as can be seen in this quote by U.S. Marine Corps Lieutenant Colonel L.B. Fuller, which appeared in a joint U.S. Marine Corps/U.S. Army report dated 12 December 1942 and titled *Notes on Jungle Warfare*: 'I wish I had the M1 rifle, and when we get relieved form Guadalcanal, I am going to make every effort to get one.'

A U.S. Army wartime publication for frontline soldiers, labeled *Combat Lessons No. 1*, contains this extract regarding infantry weapons employed in jungle warfare during the fighting in New Georgia by the 43rd Infantry Division:

> The M1 rifle is doubtless the best all-around weapon possessed by our troops. Its serviceability under existing campaign conditions is excellent. Ammunition supply was adequate, since the rifle was normally fired only at observed targets. The Japs possessed a number of our M1 rifles, apparently considering them a superior weapon to their own.

By the close of the Second World War, the Springfield Armory, in conjunction with the civilian firm of Winchester, managed to build over 4 million M1 rifles.

Approximately 8,000 were modified into a sniper rifle designated the M1C, some of which saw use in the Pacific during the last year of the war.

An M1 Garand Competitor

As already noted, there were competitors to the semi-automatic M1 rifle in the run-up to America's official entry into the Second World War. The most promising was a semi-automatic rifle, chambered for .30-06 caliber round, designed by Melvin M. Johnson, Jr., a junior U.S. Marine Corps reserve officer.

Despite the U.S. Army having already adopted the M1 rifle in 1936, the Johnson designed a semi-automatic rifle that generated enough interest to be tested by the Ordnance Department in late 1939, but in their opinion it offered no clear advantage over the M1 rifle, the same conclusion the U.S. Marine Corps reached in late 1940.

With America's official entry into the Second World War, and because the U.S. Army had priority over the U.S. Marine Corps in the issuing of the M1 rifle, it was decided in early 1942 that there was a pressing need for a semi-automatic rifle for the newly-formed Marine First Parachute Battalion. This resulted in a small number of the Johnson-designed semi-automatic rifles being acquired and used in combat in 1942. By this time, the weapon designer was referring to it as the Model of 1941 Johnson Rifle. Despite the designation, the rifle was never officially adopted by the American military, and those in use with the U.S. Marine Corps were quickly replaced by the M1 rifle.

Carbine

Following the First World War, the Ordnance Department began to think about the need for a new rifle, lighter in weight than the M1903 and firing a less power-ful cartridge than the .30-06. It was intended to be a replacement for the M1911A1 and to be employed by officers, and those who manned crew-served weapons like mortars and machine guns. Nothing came of the idea until early 1938, when the infantry branch asked the Ordnance Department to develop a full-automatic carbine weighing 5lbs or less, chambered to fire a yet-to-be designed and built intermediate-power .30 caliber cartridge.

The Ordnance Department set up a definite requirement for a new carbine in the fall of 1940 and tasked Winchester to work on the development of a new .30 caliber cartridge for that weapon. Winchester quickly submitted for testing a new rimless cartridge based on one of its existing designs in November 1940. Testing went well and the new cartridge was ordered into production.

The Ordnance Department had asked a number of civilian firms other than Winchester to submit their proposed carbine designs for testing during the summer of 1941, but none made the grade. In a second round of testing conducted in early September 1941, Winchester was asked to submit a candidate carbine. The

Winchester prototype carbine outperformed every other weapon submitted for testing, and by the end of September 1941 was standardized as the Carbine, Caliber .30, M1.

By the time the Ordnance Department adopted the Winchester carbine, it had dropped the requirement for a full-automatic carbine. The new Winchester carbine, commonly referred to as the 'M1 carbine', was a semi-automatic weapon. A model of the M1 carbine was eventually built that could fire semi-automatic or full automatic, but it did not see service during the Second World War.

As the Ordnance Department was well aware that Winchester could never hope to build as many M1 carbines as would be needed, they contracted with a number of other civilian firms to construct the weapon. By the end of the Second World War there were ten companies building the M1 carbine, with a combined total of 6 million constructed. Besides the U.S. Army, the M1 carbine was widely used by the U.S. Marine Corps during the conflict.

A single modified version of the M1 carbine was introduced into service by the Ordnance Department during the Second World War, the M1A1. It was identical to the M1 model except for its folding stock. It was intended for use by the U.S. Army's airborne forces, where compactness was of key importance.

In combat use, the M1 carbine received very mixed reviews. Soldiers and marines appreciated its light weight and compact shape. In a U.S. Army publication titled *Combat Lessons No. 3* appears this comment by Lieutenant S.C. Murray and Colonel Horace O. Cushman on intelligence patrols in the jungle: 'The carbine was used in preference to the M1 rifle since it is lighter and easier to carry through the heavy jungle growth.'

The small size and light weight of the M1 carbine were considered unimportant by many American soldiers and Marines, who sometimes decried its reliability and lack of stopping power in combat. In a March 1945 U.S. Army report is an example of the latter view with an American soldier commenting: 'The carbine is definitely not liked, because of its numerous stoppages. Also the slug has very little impact and killing ability, or power.'

A U.S. Army wartime publication for frontline soldiers, titled *Combat Lessons No. 5* contains this extract describing the efforts that some officers went through to make their men understand that the M1 carbine had limitations that they had to be aware of before going into combat:

> Great stress was laid on the proper use of the carbine by Lieutenant Colonel F.O. Hortell of the 45th Infantry Division as a result of operations at Anzio [Italy] in March [1944]. When the carbine is used properly, in lieu of the pistol, it becomes a dangerous and accurate weapon, but when it is used in place of the M1 rifle, a grave mistake has been made …

The Bayonet

The most primitive killing weapon in the hands of American infantrymen during the Second World War was the bayonet. Despite the fact that millions were built and untold thousands of them were issued to American soldiers and marines during the worldwide conflict, only a miniscule number were ever used to kill an enemy combatant. Most saw employment as utility knifes. In spite of this fact, the American military believed very strongly at the time that all men issued the bayonet had to master its use to gain confidence in their battlefield prowess.

U.S. Army General George S. Patton would state in a letter of instruction, dated 3 April 1944, to the senior commanders of the Third Army his feeling regarding the use of the bayonet:

> Few men are killed by the bayonet; many are scared of it. Bayonets should be fixed when the firefight starts. Bayonets must be sharpened by the individual soldier. The German hates the bayonet and is inferior to our men with it. Our men should know this.

Axis military success in the early part of the Second World War, which officially began on 1 September 1939, resulted in an American military build-up. As part of this increase in size, the U.S. Army Ordnance Department had anticipated a need for more bayonets and had arranged with a number of civilian contractors to begin production of a new more cheaply-made M1905 Bayonet to lower costs and speed up production.

Production of this new second generation M1905 Bayonet did not begin in earnest until September 1942. The second-generation version of the M1905 Bayonet featured plastic grips in place of the original wooden grips seen on the first generation version.

From a joint U.S. Marine Corps and U.S. Army report dated 12 December 1942 and titled *Notes on Jungle Warfare* appears this quote by Corporal Fred Carter, Company I, Fifth Marines: 'I have been charged twice by the Japs in bayonet charges. Our Marines can out-bayonet them and I know our Army men will do the same.'

In a 1 May 1945, U.S. Army report titled *Battle Experiences Against the Japanese*, done to tell U.S. Army soldiers being prepared to be transported to the Pacific how to fight the Japanese, is this passage from somebody who had already seen combat against them. He noted the sometime usefulness of the bayonet:

> We used the bayonet very little. When you have a loaded rifle, why stop to stick somebody when you can simply pull the trigger? Sometimes, however, the bayonet is useful. In one case eighteen or twenty Japs got out of a pocket and started to run to the rear. A patrol was sent out to kill them. The Japs didn't know they were coming and got strung out. The patrol leader used

exceptionally good sense. When the patrol caught up with the Japs, they decided not to fire on them but instead, starting with the rearmost enemy, killed them one or two at a time with bayonets.

Rebuilt and New Bayonets

With the ever-increasing number of vehicles entering American military service in the lead-up to America's official entry into the Second World War, it soon became apparent that the impressive 16-inch knife blade of the first and second generation M1905 Bayonet, with its 4-inch hilt, was impractical within the tight confines of vehicles. This resulted in some examples of the bayonet having their tips shortened by 6 inches as an experiment. Testing showed it to be a workable solution, and the 10-inch shortened version of the M1905 Bayonet was ordered into production as the M1 Bayonet in February 1943, with the first units coming off the production line in April 1943.

From a U.S. Army report from April 1944 and titled *Report of the New Weapon Board* appears this passage regarding the M1 bayonet: 'The new short M1 bayonet for the rifle is preferred to the old long bayonet. No breakage difficulty with this bayonet was reported. It should be remembered, however, that this bayonet has not seen extensive use in either theater [Sicily and Italy], as there has been little hand-to-hand combat.'

Production of the second-generation M1905 Bayonet ended in May 1943. It was then reclassified as 'Limited Standard', meaning it could be used if the new standardized M1 Bayonets were not available or the inventory of the weapon was exhausted. At the same time, the Ordnance Department contracted with a number of civilian firms to modify many of the older bayonets, both first and second generation, by grinding 6 inches from the knife blade and then giving them new tips. Some unmodified 1905 Bayonets, with the original 16-inch knife blade, lasted in service until the end of the Second World War.

When the American military placed the M1 carbine into service, it originally had no provisions for mounting a bayonet. Due to its small size, the existing bayonets were ill-suited for the role. It was decided by the Ordnance Department to employ a modified M3 trench knife, which had a 6.7-inch knife blade, on the carbine as a bayonet. In this configuration, it was designated the M4 Bayonet-Knife and built between July 1944 and August 1945. A least one U.S. Army report mentioned that there was little interest in a carbine bayonet from the user community fighting in Italy.

Combat Knives

Another edged weapon in the American military arsenal during the Second World War, which no doubt killed even fewer enemy soldiers than the bayonet, was the combat knife. There were none in the inventory when the United States officially entered into the Second World War. Due to requests from the user community, the Ordnance Department went back into their storage warehouses and pulled out some of their leftover First World War era M1918 Trench Knifes.

As a wartime replacement for the M1918 Trench Knife, the Ordnance Department developed a new combat knife, which was standardized in January 1943 as the Trench Knife, M3. It, in turn, was eventually superseded by the M4 Bayonet-Knife, intended for mounting on a new semi-automatic carbine.

The U.S. Marine Corps adopted the Mark 2 fighting and utility knife in late 1942. It had a 7-inch blade and 5-inch hilt. Despite being built by a variety of civilian firms, the unofficial nickname of the weapon became 'Kabar' because those built by the Union Cutlery Company had been marked on the blades with the firm's trademark name 'KA-BAR'.

An interesting observation on the use of combat knifes and bayonets appears in a joint U.S. Army and U.S. Marine Corps report dated 12 December 1942 and titled *Notes on Jungle Warfare*. In that report, U.S. Marine Corps Platoon Sergeant George E. Aho states: 'In our training for this jungle warfare we had a great deal of work in hand-to-hand individual combat, use of the knife, jujitsu, etc. With the exception of bayonet fighting, we have not used this work. I have been in many battles since I hit this island [Guadalcanal] and I have never seen anybody use it.'

Shotguns

A less well known individual weapon employed in small numbers during the Second World War by American infantrymen was the semi-automatic combat shotgun. Due to its limited range, it was primarily employed by the marines in the Pacific, where the nature of the terrain led them to be in much closer contact with the enemy than typically found in the Europe.

Prior to America's official entry into the Second World War, the Ordnance Department evaluated its inventory of combat shotguns and found it lacking. It quickly issued contracts to a number of civilian shotgun builders to supply some of their non-militarized models, and in the case of Winchester, brand new units of their First World War era Trench Gun (shotgun), Model of 1917, and another designated the Model 12.

After the First World War, the Ordnance Department dropped the label 'trench gun' and began referring to all militarized shotguns as 'riot guns'. However, the name trench gun remains the more commonly accepted name for the weapons. The Second World War U.S. Marine Corps divisional table of organization (TO&E) called for 306 trench guns. They would often see use in protecting machine gun positions at night from Japanese infiltrators, and help to clear Japanese soldiers from cave defensive positions.

Grenades

Another infantry weapon that saw a great deal of use during the Second World War with the American military, was the hand grenade, the most widely employed being designated the Hand, Fragmentation, Mark II. While it resembled its First World War predecessor, the cast iron Mark I, the cast iron Mark II had a more potent high explosive filler, which generated more fragments (200) upon detonation then the older Mark I. The Mark II was supplemented in service with the American military by the improved Hand, Fragmentation, Mark IIA1.

A couple of interesting comments on hand grenades appear in a 12 December 1942 joint U.S. Marine Corps/U.S. Army report on jungle fighting: 'Some of our new men were so scared of our hand grenades when they were first issued, that they jammed down the cotter pin. Then later, in action, they could not pull the pin.' In the same report, Platoon Sergeant H.R. Strong, Company A, Fifth Marines mentioned something he observed: 'Some of my men thought their hand grenades were too heavy. They tossed them aside when no one was looking. Later, they would have given six month's pay for one hand grenade.'

From a late war U.S. Army report appears this comment regarding the use of hand grenades by Sergeant Homer A. East: 'Whenever possible at night we use hand grenades rather than small arms. Hand grenades don't give away our positions.' From the same report appears this warning about the use of hand grenades in combat: 'Men should be taught to remove grenades from pockets and put them in handy holes when occupying positions. We have had several exploded when the men were hit.'

There was also the M15 WP (white phosphorus) grenade mainly intended as a smoke producing agent, but it was also widely employed as an antipersonnel weapon. In the same 1 May 1945 U.S. Army report is this comment on the usefulness of the M15 WP in combat: 'The white phosphorus grenade was found particularly useful against pillboxes and caves. Its incendiary effect, as well as the choking effect of its smoke, made it effective where other grenades failed.'

In addition to the Mark II and Mark IIA1 fragmentation grenades and the M15 WP grenade, there was the less known Mark III and Mark IIIA1 offensive grenades. Rather than having metal bodies, they consisted of a pressed fiber body with sheet metal ends, containing TNT. Their intended purpose was to generate a concussive effect within enclosed spaces. From a U.S. Army report dated May 1, 1945: 'Do not run down the offensive grenade. Take plenty. They will blow a Jap apart in a dugout when he could escape the fragments of a fragmentation grenade.'

Grenade Launchers

The Mark I fragmentation grenade could be thrown on average only 44 yards. To extend the range of the weapon, the Ordnance Department had adopted a French Army grenade launcher during the First World War that would remain in American military service until the 1920s, when the M1 and M2 grenade launchers replaced it in service. Both new rifle grenade launchers, as with the original French model, clamped on the end of a rifle's barrel, and increased the range of the later Mark II fragmentation grenade to approximately 165 yards.

The M1 grenade launcher was intended for use with the 1903 rifle and the M2 with the American version of the Enfield rifle. As the latter rifle saw almost no combat use during the Second World War, the M2 grenade launcher was seldom employed other than in training.

In U.S. Army publication *Combat Lessons No. 5* is this quote by Private First Class Paul Horgan, 30th Infantry Division, Normandy, France: 'The M1 grenade launcher is really a perfect weapon. We wiped out two armored cars at about 175 yards with one round apiece from four M1s. The hits tore holes 6–8 inches in diameter in the sides, killing the men inside. One shell hit a gas tank and the car blew up.'

As the M1 rifle and the M1 carbine replaced the 1903 rifle during the Second World War, the Ordnance Department had to design grenade launchers for the new rifles. The M1 rifle received the M7 grenade launcher and the M1 carbine the M8 grenade launcher.

The M7 grenade launcher was not a complete success in combat because once it was fitted to the M1 rifle it could no longer function as a semi-automatic weapon. This design issue caused the M1903 rifle, when fitted with the M1 grenade launcher, to remain in service with the American military long after the M1 rifle had superseded the M1903 rifle in infantry units. A new grenade launcher designated the M7A1, which would have allowed the M1 rifle to fire in semi-automatic mode, was not fielded until July 1945, too late to see action.

The M8 grenade launcher for the M1 carbine was very popular during the Second World War as, unlike the M1 rifle, it could be fired in its semi-automatic mode when fitted with its grenade launcher, but the heavy recoil generated by the firing of a rifle grenade sometimes damaged the weapon. An example of this problem appears in an U.S. Army report from April 1944 titled *Report of the New Weapon Board*: '… It is suggested that the theaters be given this information so that it will be fully understood that the practice of launching grenades in the carbine is an expedient and that the carbine was not designed for this purpose.'

Grenade Launcher Rounds

The M1, M7, and M8 grenade launchers could fire a variety of rounds. These included the M9 antitank rifle grenade and the improved M9A1 version. In a late war U.S. Army report from Europe appears this passage regarding other uses of the antitank rifle grenades:

> We used antitank rifle grenades effectively against personnel in town fighting. When we heard the Germans coming down the street in the dark we fired at

the sound, bouncing the grenades off the pavement and the walls of buildings. We found a number of dead Germans in the street the next morning.

Not everybody was happy with the M9A1 antitank rifle grenade, as seen in this passage from a report by the U.S. Army 37th Infantry Division taking part in the Bougainville Campaign (November 1943 through December 1943): 'Rifle grenade (AT M9A1), used in the Hill 700 fight, were not satisfactory. Against one pillbox only one of sixteen propelling cartridges exploded.'

Besides the antitank rifle grenades, there was the M17 impact fragmentation grenade, which was a standard Mark II fragmentation grenade attached to an adapter that held it in place when fitted to the grenade launcher. In addition, there was a white phosphorus (WP) rifle grenade and a number of colored smoke rifle grenades. Soldiers and marines also discovered that the 60mm mortar round could be fired from the M1 grenade launcher with a little jury-rigging.

From a U.S. Army report covering the period between July 1944 and April 1945 in Europe appears this description of what one unit did with their M1 grenade launchers:

> We get effective time fire [air bursts] with white phosphorus and fragmentation rifle grenades. A grenade, with the pin in, is placed in the grenade adapter and pushed all the way down on the launcher. As soon as the gunner is ready to fire, the pin is pulled. By inclining the rifle at about a 40 degree angle, a burst at a height of about 8–10 feet can be obtained at a range of 150 yards.

Submachine Guns

One of the best-known American infantry weapons to come out of the Second World War was the 'Thompson submachine gun'. The history of the weapon dates back to the First World War, when a U.S. Army Ordnance Department officer named John Taliaferro Thompson first conceived of a compact full-automatic, firing the short-range .45 caliber pistol cartridge, as a trench-clearing weapon. Thompson was also the person who coined the term 'submachine gun'.

Following the First World War, Thompson, now a civilian, went to the Auto-Ordnance Corporation to market his submachine gun design, now labeled the Thompson Submachine Gun, Model of 1921. Despite the favorable impressions made on the Ordnance Department during testing of the weapon in the early 1920s, no production orders resulted. However, a few hundred were bought by the U.S. Marine Corps on an *ad-hoc* basis. It was never formally accepted into service by the U.S. Marine Corps, and was employed by them during the interwar period with great effect in various low-intensity operations in a number of Third World countries.

It was not until 1928 that the U.S. Navy placed an official order for 500 units of the weapon on behalf of the U.S. Marine Corps. Reflecting some minor design changes, it became the U.S. Navy Model of 1928. The U.S. Army acquired a small number of them in 1932 as a limited procurement item for testing by the Cavalry Branch.

The Cavalry Branch was actually waiting for the M1 rifle to be issued and saw the Thompson Submachine Gun, Model of 1921 as a stop-gap weapon. However, once they tested the new M1 rifle, it was clear that the more compact Model of 1921 was a better choice. This led to the weapon being standardized in 1938 as the Sub-machine Gun, Caliber .45, Model 1928A1 and ordered in ever larger numbers.

Between 1940 and 1943, approximately 500,000 units of the Submachine Gun, Caliber .45, Model 1928A1 were built. To speed up production of the weapon, two simplified versions were also built during the Second World War; the Submachine Gun, Caliber .45, M1, beginning in 1942, and the subsequent Submachine Gun, .45, M1A1 in 1943.

From the jungles of New Georgia comes this passage regarding the usefulness of the Thompson submachine gun with the U.S. Army 43d Infantry Division: 'In spite of its handicap of sounding like a Jap .25 caliber light machine gun, the Thompson submachine gun proved very satisfactory for specialized personnel such as linemen, artillery forward observers, vehicle drivers, and reconnaissance personnel. Its limited range made it especially useful in combat in rear areas.'

From a March 1945 U.S. Army report comes a wartime impression of the Thompson submachine gun. Platoon Sergeant Jack Bradner: 'Our TSMG [Thompson Submachine Gun] has greater accuracy than the German "burp gun".'

In a 1 May 1945 U.S. Army report titled *Battle Experiences Against the Japanese* comes this comment from a marine assigned to the 7th Marine Regiment on Guadalcanal about the Thompson submachine gun: 'The Thompson submachine gun is very effective, because Japs usually execute their attacks en masses.'

A Cheaper Alternative

Due to the complexity and cost of the various versions of the Thompson submachine gun, the Ordnance Department began looking in early 1941 for a simpler and less costly submachine gun. The eventual answer to that search was contracted for in December 1942 and designated the Submachine Gun, Caliber .45, M3. Reflecting its similarity to a tool employed for lubricating automobiles of the era, it was nicknamed the 'Grease Gun'.

The M3 submachine gun as designed could only be fired in full automatic mode. It did not have the conventional wooden stock and handgrip found on the various models of the Thompson submachine gun. Instead, it had only a retractable wire stock.

In addition to its then unconventional appearance, which put off many soldiers and marines, there were also a number of minor design problems with the early pro-duction M3 submachine guns. Once the early design problems were resolved by the

Ordnance Department the M3 Grease Gun was gradually accepted by American soldiers and marines, but never equaled the popularity of the Thompson submachine gun.

From a couple of different U.S. Army reports appear these conflicting opinions on the M3 Grease Gun. In an April 1944 U.S. Army report titled *Report of the New Weapon Board* about the combat impression of small arms employed in the Italian Theater: 'This item was immediately popular, as would be expected, and was accepted as a timely answer to the German Schmeisser [MP-40].'

From a lieutenant colonel in a March 1945 U.S. Army report comes the opposing view of the M3 Grease Gun: 'American guns and small arms of all types are superior to German guns and small arms in that they are of better construction and material. The possible exception might be the submachine gun M3. This gun is cheaply and crudely made, and does not compare with the Schmeisser Machine Pistol [MP-40].'

By the war's end, over 600,000 units of the M3 Grease Gun had come off of American factory floors. An improved and simplified model was the Submachine Gun, Caliber .45, M3A1 approved for production in December 1944. However, few saw combat before the Second World War ended.

A Stop-Gap Submachine Gun

With the outbreak of the Second World War, and the assumption by many that the United States would eventually be pulled into the conflict, some saw a business opportunity. One such person was Eugene G. Reising, who applied for a patent on a new submachine gun design in June 1940. The Ordnance Department quickly sought out the Reising submachine gun to see if it could meet the needs of the U.S. Army.

Ordnance Department testing of the Reising submachine gun, which fired a .45 caliber pistol cartridge, led the U.S. Army to reject the weapon and continue to depend on the Thompson submachine. Since the production of the Thompson submachine gun could barely meet the demands of the U.S. Army and the American government's various lend-lease commitments, the U.S. Marine Corps decided as a stop-gap measure to adopt the Reising submachine gun in early 1942 as a strictly supplementary weapon until a more suitable submachine gun could be acquired.

In U.S. Marine Corps service, the original version of the weapon was designated the Model 50. A later model, intended for use by the newly-formed Marine First Parachute Battalion, had a folding wire stock, and was labeled the Model 55. Combat use by the U.S. Marine Corps early in the Second World War led to the Reising submachine gun quickly acquiring a reputation as an unreliable weapon, besieged by numerous design issues. It was disposed of by the U.S. Marine Corps by 1943.

From a private collection comes this picture of the Pistol, Caliber .45 Model 1911A1. The leather holster for the weapon was designated the Holster, Pistol, Caliber .45, M7. Also seen in the picture are a loaded magazine for the weapon and its standard two magazine belt pouch. *(Martin Morgan collection)*

Shown on a range during the Second World War is a young marine learning how to properly shoot his Pistol, Caliber .45 Model 1911A1. The most challenging part of mastering the 1911A1 was the trigger squeeze, which was difficult to apply when it was loaded. The weapon weighed 2.76 pounds with a full seven round magazine. *(NA)*

In this slightly out of focus wartime picture is a U.S. Marine Corps two-man antitank rocket launcher team, with the loader in the foreground armed with a Pistol, Caliber .45 Model 1911A1. These crew-served weapons teams were typically issued pistols instead of rifles as they had so much other equipment to transport on the battlefield. (NA)

A group of U.S. Army soldiers are seen preparing to breach a door. The man in the middle of the picture is armed with a Pistol, Caliber .45 Model 1911A1. In the often extremely close fighting that is so characteristic of urban warfare, a pistol could prove more useful than many other types of small arms. (NA)

An American soldier lies in wait for some unseen threat. He is armed with a Pistol, Caliber .45 Model 1911A1. The initial model of the weapon was designated the Automatic Pistol, Caliber .45, Model of 1911. The use of the word 'automatic' in the weapon's original designation was technically incorrect, as it was a semi-automatic weapon that required a trigger pull for each shot. (NA)

The Pistol, Caliber .45 Model 1911A1 remained in the American military postwar. Pictured is a marine armed with an M1911A1 on a target range in the 1980s. Such is the recoil of the M1911A1 that it is typical for a shooter's firing arm to have a vertical movement of 6–8 inches upon firing each shot. (DOD)

(*Above*) A First World War picture showing U.S. Army soldiers wearing gas masks and pointing their bayonet-equipped bolt-action rifles, designated as the Magazine Rifle, Caliber .30, Model of 1903, down range. The rifle is best known as the 'Springfield', 'Springfield .03', or just the '.03'. Later, it would be referred to as the M1903 Springfield rifle, although it was also built by the Rock Island Arsenal. (*NA*)

(*Opposite above*) Pictured is a U.S. Army infantryman during a post-First World War training exercise armed with the bolt-action M1903 Springfield rifle. With the American military shrinking in size following the First World War, also referred to as 'The War to End All Wars', and a large number of M1903 Springfield rifles left over from that conflict, production of the weapon ceased in 1927. (*NA*)

(*Opposite below*) From the beginning of its production run prior to the First World War, up through 1927, the bolt-action M1903 Springfield rifle was built to a very high standard of workmanship, including a walnut stock with finger grooves, as seen here in this prewar picture of a squad of U.S. Army infantrymen during a training exercise. (*NA*)

In this photograph of American soldiers can be seen two different models of the bolt-action M1903 Springfield rifle. The soldier in the foreground is taking aim with his Rifle, Caliber .30, M1913 (modified), which was re-designated as the Rifle, Caliber .30 Model 1903A3 in May 1942. The soldier in the background is armed with a scope-fitted version of the weapon designated as the Rifle, Caliber .30 Model M1903A4 (Sniper's). (NA)

(Opposite page) The design of bolt-action M1903 Springfield rifle was simplified upon America's official entry into the Second World War. A key external feature of the wartime-built 1903 Springfield is the lack of finger grooves in the stock, as seen in this photograph. The Ordnance Department initially referred to this version of the weapon as the Rifle, Caliber .30, M1913 (modified). (NA)

A young Marine takes aim with his Rifle, Caliber .30 Model M1903A4 (Sniper's). The scope fitted to the weapon was designated the M73B1 Telescopic Sight by the Ordnance Department. It was a military version of a civilian 2.2 × telescopic scope with a crosshair reticle designed and built by the firm of Weaver. (NA)

(*Opposite above*) Pictured during a training exercise are two American soldiers armed with the Rifle, Caliber .30, Model of 1917, better known as the 'Enfield'. It was a First World War era bolt-action rifle. It was pressed into service as a stopgap training weapon early in the Second World War. (*NA*)

(*Above*) The eventual replacement for the bolt-action M1903 Springfield rifle in the American military during the Second World War was the Semiautomatic Rifle, Caliber .30, M1 seen here in the arms of a U.S. Army soldier during a pre-war training exercise. Those who were issued the weapon typically referred to it as either as the 'M1' or the 'M1 rifle'. Hereafter in the text it will be referred to as the M1 rifle. (*NA*)

(*Opposite below*) The business end of the gas-operated M1 rifle is aimed at an imaginary target in this posed photograph. The M1 rifle is commonly referred to by postwar history buffs and weapons collectors as the 'Garand'. The weapon was the only semi-automatic rifle in general issue to any of the armies that participated in the Second World War. (*NA*)

A U.S. Army infantryman armed with an M1 rifle stands over the corpse of a German soldier he may have killed in combat. In contrast to a standard wartime bolt action rifle that might be capable of a rate of fire of 10–15 rounds a minute, the M1 rifle was capable of firing 20–30 aimed shots per minute. *(NA)*

Two U.S. Army infantrymen armed with the M1 rifle await the enemy in a hastily dug foxhole. The M1 rifle fired several types of ammunition that were identified by individual markings. The most common round was referred to as Ball, M2, which was unpainted and was intended for use against personnel and unarmored targets. (NA)

A U.S. Army infantryman, armed with an M1 rifle in the prone firing position, sports an improvised snow camouflage suit. The Ball, M2 cartridge for the weapon had an approximate maximum range of 3,500 yards, which is not the same as effective range. Muzzle velocity of the M1 rifle ranged between 2,600-2,800 feet per second. (NA)

(*Above*) A marine sitting on top of a pile of Japanese ammunition boxes with his 9.5-pound M1 rifle takes aim at some distant target. In battle, the effectiveness of small arms fire at anything other than close range depended upon the accuracy of range estimation by the user. A trained rifleman, according to a wartime U.S. Army manual, should have been able to accurately estimate ranges at up to 600 yards. (*NA*)

(*Opposite above*) In his one-man foxhole, a U.S. Army soldier takes aim with his M1 rifle. A standard eight round clip is affixed to the weapon's sling for ease of access. The rear sight on the M1 rifle was adjusted for range by an elevating knob that had numbered graduations that varied between 200 and 1,200 yards. The effective range of the weapon was considered to be 500 yards. (*NA*)

(*Opposite below*) A U.S. Army infantry squad warily walks through a village somewhere in Western Europe. Two of the soldiers are armed with the M1 rifle, with one of the two having acquired a German military pistol, as is evident by the non-issue holster on his cartridge belt. The M1 rifle had a length of 43.6 inches, with the barrel being 24 inches. (*NA*)

A marine armed with an M1 rifle carefully scans the tree above his location for enemy snipers. It was discovered in the Pacific that the high moisture content of jungle areas would cause the wooden stocks on the rifle to swell and in turn pinch the weapon's firing mechanisms. The answer was to apply a light coat of raw linseed oil to the wooden stock to relieve any binding. (NA)

Taking cover behind a palm tree, a marine aims his M1 rifle at his battlefield opponents. Besides the standard Ball, M2 ammunition, there was also another round designated Armor-Piercing, M2. It had a black painted bullet tip. It was intended for use against lightly armored vehicles, protective shelters, and enemy personnel. (NA)

Two M1 rifle armed U.S. Army soldiers are shown sitting on a captured German defensive work. Besides their standard issue cartridge belts, both infantrymen shown have cloth ammunition bandoleers looped around their upper torsos. The infantryman on the left hand side of the picture has attached two eight round clips to one of the cloth ammunition bandoleers he is wearing. (NA)

Jumping out of a wooden M2 assault boat are U.S. Army infantrymen armed with the M1 rifle. The M1 rifle was made up of about seventy parts, the mass production of which was an exacting process requiring the parts to be cut and machined to very rigid tolerances to ensure that it worked reliably when called upon. (NA)

A U.S. Army soldier cradles his M1 rifle. It had an internal magazine that was loaded by inserting a pre-loaded eight round clip. The entire clip had to be fired and automatically ejected before the weapon could be reloaded. Besides the Springfield Armory, the civilian firm of Winchester was awarded a contract to build the M1 rifle during the Second World War. (NA)

Besides being used to kill enemy soldiers, the M1 rifle could be used for other purposes; it was sometimes employed to mark the location of a deceased soldier or marine. In this picture we see the M1 rifle of a wounded marine being used to support an IV bottle as a friend or medic attends to him. (NA)

In need of a defensive weapon that offered both more firepower and greater range than the M1911A1 issued to officers, crew-served weapons teams, and rear echelon support troops, the Ordnance Department adopted the Carbine, Caliber .30 M1 shown here, hereafter referred to as the M1 carbine. Fully loaded with a fifteen round detachable box magazine and with sling attached, it weighed less than six pounds. (NA)

(*Above*) Two U.S. Army soldiers, one being armed with an M1 carbine, look out from the bottom floor of a building. Below them lies the corpse of a German soldier killed in a previous engagement. By 1943, the Ordnance Department had contracted with ten civilian firms to build the M1 carbine and 3 million were constructed that year, still a million short of the requirement. (*NA*)

(*Opposite page*) An M1 carbine armed U.S. Army infantryman stands at the ready in his foxhole. Prior to the attack on Pearl Harbor, it was anticipated that the American military had a requirement for 886,698 units of the M1 carbine. Following Pearl Harbor, plans were drawn up that called for the production of 1 million M1 carbines by the end of 1942. However, production bottlenecks led to only 115,000 being built in 1942. (*NA*)

A U.S. Army infantryman is shown looking up from his foxhole at some aerial activity while eating food rations. By his side lies his M1 carbine. The gas-operated semi-automatic weapon had an overall length of 35.6 inches with a barrel length of 18 inches. Firing the standard ball ammunition, the M1 carbine had a muzzle velocity of 1,970 feet per second. (NA)

Armed with an M1 carbine, a marine carefully looks into an enemy dugout for any sign of occupancy. Big advantages of the M1 carbine over the M1911A1 were its effective range of 300 yards, and the ease with which the handling of the weapon was taught to those to whom it was issued. By way of comparison, the M1911A1 had an effective range of only 50 yards, and took a great deal of practice to master. (NA)

A marine armed with an M1 carbine is shown looking over the corpses of two Japanese soldiers. The U.S. Marine Corps did not adopt the weapon until after Pearl Harbor. After only a short time in service, some marine officers were so impressed with the weapon's capabilities that they suggested it completely replace the M1911A1, and all the submachine guns then in service. (NA)

(*Above*) Peering out from his camouflage foxhole is a marine armed with the M1 carbine, minus its 15-round detachable magazine. Notice the weapon's lack of a bayonet lug, which did not begin appearing on new production M1 carbines until very late in the war. Postwar, most Second World War M1 carbines had the bayonet lug fitted when they were refurbished for future use. (*NA*)

(*Opposite above*) A small group of U.S. Army officers and non-commissioned officers armed with the M1 carbine are shown conferring over several maps at what must be some type of command post, based on the overhead cover erected behind them. The M1 carbine was authorized for officers up to the rank of major in lieu of the M1911A1. (*NA*)

(*Opposite below*) A marine is shown engaging the enemy with his M1 carbine. In the foreground are dead Japanese soldiers. Infantrymen who substituted the M1 carbine for their M1 rifles sometimes came to regret their decision when confronted by the fact that the lower muzzle velocity of the carbine and smaller caliber bullet lacked the stopping power of the more hard-hitting M1 rifle. (*NA*)

A U.S. Army soldier armed with an M1 carbine is shown guarding a room full of prisoners. American soldiers were instructed to separate all military prisoners into three groups: officers, noncommissioned officers, and privates. Due to the Japanese military code of honor, the taking of prisoners in the Pacific was far less frequent, as the Japanese soldiers preferred death before surrender. (NA)

A marine poses with his M1 rifle fitted with an M1905 bayonet. From a U.S. Marine Corps manual appears this extract describing the bayonet's usefulness: 'Often a determined enemy cannot be dislodged by fire alone, and must be driven from his position by hand-to hand combat. The bayonet or the threat of the bayonet is the ultimate factor in every assault.'

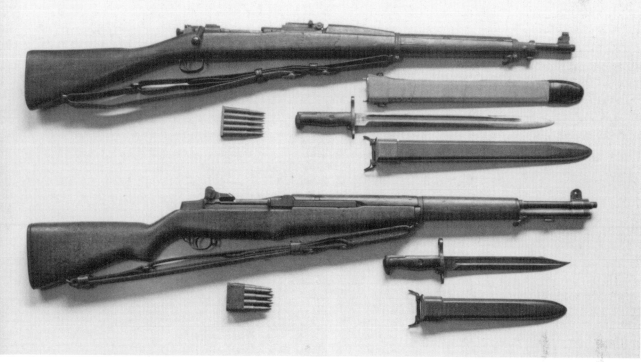

At the top of the picture is an M1903A3 rifle and an M1905 bayonet with the original pre-Second World War built leather and cotton-webbed scabbard, designated the M1910. Under it is its Second World War built plastic replacement referred to as the M3 bayonet scabbard. Below, the M1903A3 rifle is an M1 rifle displayed with the wartime built M1 bayonet and its plastic scabbard known as the M7. (USMCHC)

A young marine is shown with his M1 rifle with an M1905 bayonet fitted. According to a U.S. Marine Corps manual, the optimum environment for the employment of the bayonet was at night, on infiltration missions, and whenever secrecy was an important element of a combat mission. (NA)

(*Above*) Two marines are seen in this picture. Both are armed with the Winchester Model 12 Trench Gun. Compared to the millions of M1 rifles and M1 carbines built during the Second World War, the various shotguns employed by the American military in the conflict were built in fairly small numbers, reflecting their limited battlefield utility. (*NA*)

(*Opposite page*) A U.S. Army infantryman is shown talking on an SCR 536 radio, originally known as the 'handie talkie' and later as the 'walkie talkie'. It was the world's first military hand-held self-contained two wave radio. The soldier has an M7 plastic bayonet scabbard on his cartridge belt for his M1 bayonet. (*NA*)

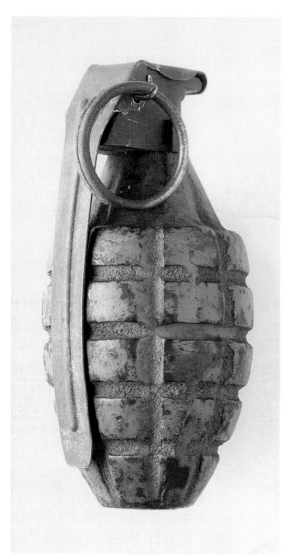

(*Above left*) Pictured is an inert example of the Fragmentation Hand Grenade Mark II. The body of the grenade was made of cast iron, painted olive drab with no markings. Its outer surface was cast with deep grooves to improve its fragmentation effect upon detonation. The weapon was widely used in the Pacific, where combat was often conducted at very short ranges. (*Martin Morgan collection*)

(*Above right*) A drill instructor demonstrates the proper manner of throwing a hand grenade from the standing position. According to a U.S. Marine Corps manual, the hand grenade should be hurled with a free and natural motion, much like a baseball. It goes on to state that it needs to be thrown with a snapping motion of the wrist just before the arm is fully extended and roll off the tips of the fingers. (*NA*)

(*Opposite page*) Marines are shown tossing grenades at the enemy. The Fragmentation Hand Grenade Mark II weighed 22.4oz and had a detonating type fuze that, when it exploded, set off the TNT filler contained within the grenade body. Detonating type fuzes typically have a time delay of four to five seconds. (*NA*)

A U.S. Army infantryman loads up a bag with Fragmentation Hand Grenade Mark IIs. Among the Mark II grenades is a single example of the larger Incendiary Grenade M14, which had a cylinder-shaped sheet steel body marked with a horizontal band. It was designed to start fires or melt the metal parts of captured enemy equipment. (NA)

Visible on the chest of this U.S. Army infantryman firing his M1 rifle at the enemy is an Incendiary Grenade M14. The 32oz grenade had a two-second delay igniting fuze, and was filled with thermite. Thermite is a mixture of chemicals that when ignited burns at an extremely high temperature. (NA)

A photograph of a U.S. Army infantryman shows two Fragmentation Hand Grenade Mark IIs on his chest attached to strings that appear to be tied to a shoulder loop on his jacket. Soldiers and marines were reminded to handle their grenades with extreme caution at all times, as their detonators contained a charge of mercury fulminate composition that was very sensitive to heat, shock, or friction. (NA)

An instructor at a U.S. Army training facility points out the various components that made up the Fragmentation Hand Grenade Mark II. During fragmentation grenade training, it was stressed that one should not release the safety lever before throwing it, and that when thrown all friendly personnel should be at least 40 yards away from the point of impact. (NA)

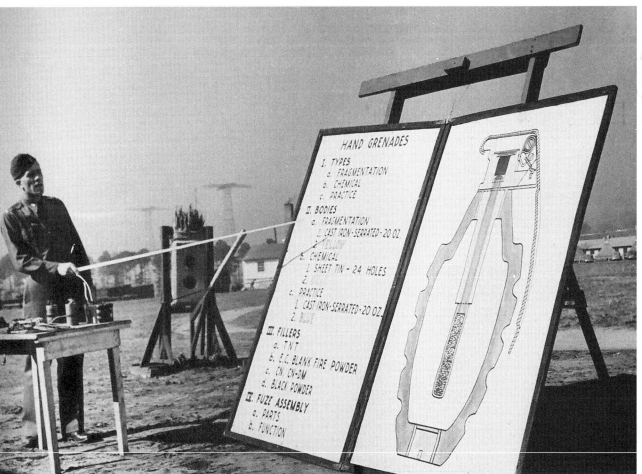

HAND GRENADES

1. TYPES
   a. FRAGMENTATION
   b. CHEMICAL
   c. PRACTICE
II. BODIES
   a. FRAGMENTATION
      1. CAST IRON-SERRATED-20 OZ.
      2. YELLOW
   b. CHEMICAL
      1. SHEET TIN - 24 HOLES
      2.
   c. PRACTICE
      1. CAST IRON-SERRATED-20 OZ.
      2. BLUE
III. FILLERS
   a. T.N.T.
   b. E.C. BLANK FIRE POWDER
   c. CN, CN-DM
   d. BLACK POWDER
IV. FUZE ASSEMBLY
   a. PARTS
   b. FUNCTION

(*Above left*) A U.S. Army soldier is shown attaching a rifle grenade designated the Grenade, Rifle, HE, AT, M9A1 to an M1903 Springfield rifle fitted with the Grenade Launcher M1. Originally envisioned as an antitank weapon by the American military, its effectiveness against heavily armored German tanks and self-propelled guns was very limited. However, it could be effective against more lightly armored vehicles. (*NA*)

(*Above right*) A marine has just fired a rifle grenade from the Grenade Launcher M7. The M7 is seen at the muzzle end of the rifle. It attached to the M1 rifle bayonet lug with a stud that fitted into the weapon's gas valve screw, and was intended to vent excess gas to prevent damage to the weapon due to recoil. The effective range of the M1 and M7 Grenade Launchers was 40–50 yards. (*NA*)

(*Opposite page*) Two U.S. Army infantrymen are shown conferring over the day's events. Both are armed with M1 rifles, with one being fitted with the Grenade Launcher M7 and mounting an M9A1 rifle grenade. An improved model of the M7 that would allow the M1 rifle to fire in full semi-automatic mode was designated the M7A1, but did not reach the field until after the Second World War. (*NA*)

A U.S. Army officer is pictured ready to fire an M9A1 rifle grenade from the Grenade Launcher M7. Attached to the rifle grenade is possibly communication wire, which could be carried over intervening obstacles by way of an unprimed grenade. The big disadvantage of the M7 is that it restricted the semi-automatic M1 rifle to only firing single shots when mounted on the weapon. (NA)

Three U.S. Army infantrymen are shown ready to breach the door of a possibly enemy occupied building. The soldier in the middle is armed with an M1 rifle fitted with the Grenade Launcher M7 and armed with an M9A1 rifle grenade. The rifle grenade weighted 1.31lbs and had a shaped charge warhead that was in theory able to penetrate up to 3 inches of armor. (NA)

Besides being able to fire the M9A1 rifle grenade, the Grenade Launcher M7 could fire the Mark II Fragmentation Grenade with the Projection Adapter M1A1, which is visible on the end of the M1 rifle pictured here. The grenade launchers M1 and M7 could not be fired with standard ball ammunition, but only a special grenade cartridge. (NA)

An elderly woman pours a glass of wine for a U.S. Army soldier. The soldier is armed with an M1 carbine fitted with the Grenade Launcher M8 developed specially for the weapon. As the gas-operated recoil system of the M1 carbine differed from that of the M1 rifle, the fitting of the M8 did not stop the weapon from firing in the semi-automatic mode. (NA)

In this pre-Second World War photograph, a soldier poses on a parked U.S. Army motorcycle and pretends to aim a weapon designated the Submachine Gun, Caliber .45, Model of 1928A1 by the Ordnance Department. It was better known to most as the 'Thompson Submachine Gun' or just the 'Tommy Gun'. (NA)

In a dramatically composed picture, a U.S. Army soldier is armed with a Model of 1928A1. It is equipped with a 50-round detachable drum magazine that first appeared on the original model of the weapon marketed as the Thompson Submachine Gun, Model of 1921, and the subsequent model ordered by the U.S. Navy as the Model of 1928. (NA)

A marine armed with Model of 1928A1 takes a break. His weapon is equipped with a 50-round drum magazine. Combat experience showed that the drum magazine rattled when shaken, and hence became unpopular among some marines, who felt it was not prudent to alert the enemy to their presence on the battlefield. (NA)

(*Above left*) The marine pictured is armed with a Model of 1928A1 equipped with a 30-round detachable box magazine. A key spotting feature of the M1918A1 and the models of the weapon that preceded it was the cocking handle on the top of the weapon's receiver and the Cutts Compensator at the end of the barrel, which was intended to keep down recoil. (*NA*)

(*Above right*) A U.S. Army soldier takes aim at a pretend enemy with his Model of 1928A1. With the official outbreak of the Second World War in September 1939, the U.S. Army became more interested in acquiring larger numbers of the Model of 1928A1. In 1939, they ordered 950, in 1940 that order was pushed up to 20,405, and in 1941, it reached 319,000 units. (*NA*)

(*Right*) The marine leading this patrol is armed with a Model of 1928A1. The Ordnance Department sought to simplify the design of the weapon to both speed up its production and lower its cost. The minor design changes were done in stages shortly after production began in 1940 and continued until production of the M1928A1 ceased in 1943. (*NA*)

A wary U.S. Army soldier looks over a hedgerow for any sign of the enemy. He is armed with the Model of 1928A1, which is evident from the Cutts Compensator at the end of the weapon's barrel. In spite of the design changes made to the weapon, the Ordnance Department designation remained the same. By 1943, a total of 562,511 units of the M1928A1 had been built. (NA)

Two marines are shown firing at the enemy. The marine in the foreground is armed with the Model of 1928A1, as can be determined by the Cutts Compensator. What is interesting in this picture is the five-pocket canvas pouch for the weapon's detachable box magazines, which attached to a standard pistol belt. (NA)

The M1928A1 was expansive and time-consuming to build. The Ordnance Department's short-term fix for the problem was the introduction of a radically redesigned version of the weapon designated as the Submachine Gun, Caliber .45, M1, an example of which is seen in the hands of the U.S. Army soldier guarding some German prisoners. (NA)

The most important external spotting features of the Submachine Gun, Caliber .45, M1, seen here in the hand of a marine, was the loss of the Cutts Compensator at the end of the barrel, and the relocation of the cocking handle from the top of the receiver to the right side of the receiver. (NA)

A marine is shown firing his Submachine Gun, Caliber .45, M1. Unlike the M1928A1, the M1 submachine gun lacked the finned barrel seen on the earlier model, which had been intended to help cool the barrel. Its removal on some late-production M1928A1 and the M1 submachine gun showed no ill effects on the weapon's effectiveness in battle. *(NA)*

(*Above*) An American soldier shows his buddy where a bullet dented his helmet. His friend is armed with a slightly improved model of the M1 submachine gun designated by the Ordnance Department as the Submachine Gun, Caliber .45 M1A1. It can be identified from the previous version by the appearance of projecting metal guards on either side of the stamped rear sight. (*NA*)

(*Opposite page*) Two members of a U.S. Army artillery forward observation team scan the area around their position for any possible targets. At the foot of the soldier in the foreground is his Submachine Gun, Caliber .45 M1A1, as is evidenced by the projecting metal guards on the rear of the weapon's receiver. (*NA*)

An American soldier armed with either an M1 or M1A1 submachine gun looks over a German 88mm antiaircraft gun destroyed by its own crew. While well thought of by many soldiers and marines and often sought out, the Thompson submachine gun series was very difficult to control in full automatic fire and hence very inaccurate at other than very close ranges. Some wartime reports quote 50 yards as being the maximum effective range of the weapon. (NA)

The result of the Ordnance Department's search for a cheaper submachine gun that consumed fewer raw materials and was faster to build in large numbers than the Thompson submachine gun series was the Submachine Gun, Caliber .45, M3, which was issued beginning in late 1943. A U.S. Army soldier is shown firing an M3 submachine gun from the cover of a large tree. (NA)

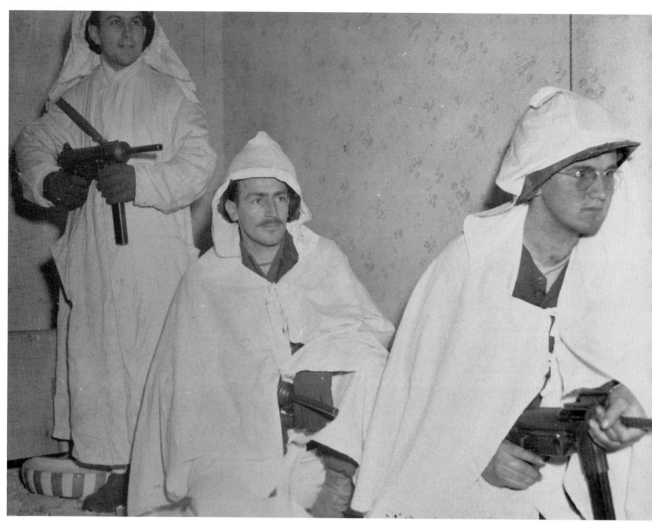

Several U.S. Army infantrymen, armed with the M3 submachine gun and wearing improvised snow suits, are shown prior to going out on patrol. The M3 cost only $21.00 to build. Compare this to the lowest wartime price of the simplified M1/M1A1 Thompson submachine gun, which came in at $45.00, in 1944. (NA)

An interesting photograph of a U.S. Army soldier armed with an M3 submachine gun that has two extra 30-round box magazines taped to the magazine already inserted in his weapon. No doubt it might have speeded up reloading the weapon, but it must have made it awkward to aim and fire. Others armed with submachine guns sometimes taped two magazines together to speed up reloading in combat. (NA)

A U.S. Army soldier sitting in the back of a Jeep aims his M3 submachine gun at two German prisoners of war sitting on the hood of the vehicle. As the M3 had far looser design parameters than the Thompson submachine series, it proved to be more reliable in the field, as it could tolerate a great deal more abuse, including mud and dust. *(NA)*

(*Above left*) A pint-sized U.S. Army soldier is shown armed with an M3 submachine gun. Despite being lighter, more compact, and more reliable than the Thompson machine gun series, many soldiers disliked its lack of finish and craftsmanship, and rejected it use. Others who overlooked its appearance found it a useful weapon in combat. (*NA*)

(*Above right*) A soldier is shown firing an M3 submachine gun during a demonstration. Unlike the Thompson submachine gun series, which had been designed from the outset to be fired in either full-automatic or semi-automatic mode, the M3 could only be fired in full automatic mode. However, its lower rate of fire meant it was easier to control when fired and hence more accurate than the Thompson submachine gun series. (*NA*)

(*Opposite page*) A marine armed with an M3 submachine gun is shown checking something belonging to a Japanese prisoner of war. As the U.S. Army sought to replace the Thompson submachine gun series with the M3 submachine gun, the U.S. Marine Corps decided to look at the weapon, and quickly decided to adopt it for its own use during the closing stages of the Second World War. (*NA*)

(*Above*) A marine poses with a Reising submachine gun labeled the Model 55, which had a metal folding stock. Another version was fitted with a conventional wooden stock and was referred to as the Model 50. The Model 50 Reising submachine gun had a compensator fitted to the end of its barrel to reduce recoil climb, as had the M1928A1 TSMG. (*NA*)

(*Opposite page*) A U.S. Army Military Policeman armed with an M3 submachine gun is shown with a captured German child soldier. To correct some design deficiencies an improved model of the M3, labeled the M3A1, showed up in service in 1945. However, only 15,469 were constructed prior to the end of the Second World War. (*NA*)

In this shot we see four very serious looking marines in the PTO, armed with Model 55 Reising submachine guns. Both models of the Reising submachine gun could use either a 20-round magazine, or the 12-round magazines seen in this photograph. The 12-round box magazine was more popular, as it was supposedly more reliable than the larger box magazine. *(NA)*

Chapter Two

Crew-Served Infantry Weapons

An extremely popular weapon with American soldiers and marines during the Second World War was the Browning Automatic Rifle, Caliber .30, M1918A2, better known as the 'BAR'. The weapon was chambered for the .30-06 cartridge, and could only be fired in full-automatic mode. The name 'Browning' in the weapon's designation referred to famous American civilian inventor, John M. Browning.

Browning had first conceived of an automatic rifle at the beginning of the twentieth century. Due to the lack of U.S. Army interest at the time, he did not pursue its development. It was not until America's entry into the First World War in 1917 that the U.S. Army identified a need for an automatic rifle. The role intended for the automatic rifle was to assist bolt-action rifle toting American soldiers and marines in crossing the intervening area between trench lines by keeping down the heads of enemy soldiers as they neared their objectives.

Of the various candidate automatic rifles submitted to the Ordnance Department for testing in 1917, it was the prototype model designed and built by John Browning that proved superior to all other contenders, and it was quickly adopted. It was originally standardized in 1917 as the Browning Machine Rifle, Model of 1918, and then quickly changed to Browning Automatic Rifle, Model of 1918.

Automatic rifles differ from machine guns as they are light enough to be held and fired by one-man, whereas machine guns are typically too heavy to be held and fired accurately by one man and require a mount to support them when firing. Automatic rifles are fed by detachable magazines, and machine guns are fed by belted ammunition.

Due to their higher rate of fire, automatic rifles become crew-served weapons, as they typically need to be supported by additional manpower to carry the ammunition required. Automatic rifles were eventually replaced in service by individual assault rifles, which made their first appearance in German military service at the tail end of the Second World War.

Based on the First World War era Browning Automatic Rifle, Model of 1918 version, two interwar variants appeared in small numbers; the first was for the Cavalry Branch of the U.S. Army known as the Browning Automatic Rifle, Model of 1922.

The second was the M1918A1, adopted in 1937. With the lead-up to America's official entry into the Second World War, the Ordnance Department authorized the final production version of the Browning Automatic Rifle, Caliber .30, M1918A2, in 1940.

The M1918A2 version of the BAR was redesigned to simplify its production to maximize the number that could be built in the shortest amount of time. The changes made to the M1918A2 variant of the BAR, included the deletion of the weapon's semi-automatic mode. The U.S. Army felt that it was no longer needed, as that role was to be assumed by the semi-automatic M1 rifle.

The first production examples of the M1918A2 were based on the conversion of existing M1918 and M1918A1 from reserve storage, of which 87,000 were on hand. This process would continue until the inventory of these weapons was exhausted. In June 1940, approximately 25,000 early model BARs, not updated to the M1918A2 standard, were transferred to England between 1940 and 1941 in a show of solidarity between the two countries.

After America's official entry into the Second World War, the Ordnance Department contracted with a number of civilian firms to build new units of the M1918A2. These included the umbrella organization known as the New England Small Arms Corporation (NESA), which encompassed six companies, with a large number of subcontractors. In total, the NESA would build 168,000 brand new M1918A2 units during the war years, with production beginning in January 1943.

International Business Machines Corporation (IBM) built 25,000 new M1918A2 units before the Ordnance Department canceled that contract so the firm could concentrate on building the M1 carbine instead.

The BAR in Combat

With a reputation as both a reliable and hard-hitting weapon, the M1918A2 was in high demand with the American military throughout the Second World War. Its potent reputation soon became known to the enemy who targeted soldiers equipped with the BARs, as is seen in this quote from a 12 December 1942 joint U.S. Marine Corps/U.S. Army report on jungle fighting: 'I think the Japanese snipers look for BAR men. No doubt about this. In one engagement, in one platoon, every BAR man was hit.'

A U.S. Army wartime publication, for frontline soldiers, labeled *Combat Lessons No. 1*, contains this extract regarding the BAR:

... It is one of our more effective weapons but must be in the hands of a trained man to be really valuable. A BAR man in one of our companies got 20 Germans "for sure" in one hour during one of their counterattacks; this was one-half the casualties his platoon inflicted.'

The BAR's Place in the Rifle Squad

In the TO&E of the U.S. Army during the Second World War every standard infantry rifle platoon of approximately forty men was subdivided into three twelve-man rifle squads equipped with a single BAR and eleven M1 rifles. In lieu of the M1 rifle, some squad leaders would arm themselves with a submachine gun or M1 carbine.

The standard twelve-man U.S. Army infantry squad was subdivided into three parts; the three-man security element known as 'Able', the three-man base-of-fire element, known as 'Baker' consisting of the automatic rifleman, armed with the BAR, the assistant automatic rifleman, and the ammunition bearer; and finally the six-man rifle-equipped maneuvering element referred to as 'Charley'. As the war went on it was not uncommon for U.S. Army infantry squads to acquire one or two additional BARs to increase their firepower.

The U.S. Marine Corps TO&E for its infantry squads dramatically changed during the war. Prior to America's official entry into the Second World War, U.S. Marine Corps infantry rifle squads consisted of only nine men: one BAR man and eight riflemen armed with the M1903 Springfield bolt-action rifles, one of whom served as the squad leader. One rifleman was assigned as the assistant automatic rifleman, carrying extra BAR magazines.

Following the Japanese attack on Pearl Harbor, the U.S. Marine Corps bumped up its infantry squad to thirteen men; one BAR man and twelve M1903 Springfield rifles, one of whom served as the squad leader. One rifleman was assigned as the assistant automatic rifleman and tasked with carrying extra BAR magazines.

Combat experience led the U.S. Marine Corps to reconfigure its infantry rifle squads again in April 1943. Instead of thirteen men they were dropped to twelve men; two armed with the BAR and the remainder armed with the M1 rifle. Many squad leaders often armed themselves with submachine guns, as did U.S. Army infantry rifle squad leaders. Two riflemen were assigned as assistant automatic riflemen.

Feedback from the field resulted in the U.S. Marine Corps redoing their infantry squad organization once again in May 1944 by adding in a third BAR, and subdividing the squad into three four-man fire teams. Within each fire team there was a rifleman assigned as the assistant automatic rifleman.

A New Johnson-Designed Weapon

Melvin M. Johnson, the designer of the semi-automatic Model of 1941 Johnson rifle employed by some specialized U.S. Marine Corps units in the early stages of the Second World War, also came up with a variation of his rifle that could fire in semi-automatic mode and in full automatic mode. Despite the inventor labeling the weapon as the Model of 1941 Johnson Light Machine Gun, it was a magazine-fed weapon and therefore the American military classified it as an automatic rifle, like the BAR.

The Model of 1941 Johnson Light Machine Gun was tested by the Ordnance Department in August 1942 and rejected as not offering any clear advantage over the BAR, which the designer had hoped he could convince the American military to replace with his weapon. The U.S. Marine Corps picked up a number of Johnson's light machine Guns in 1942 to make up for a temporary shortage of BARs in some specialized U.S. Marine Corps units. However, like the inventor's semi-automatic rifle, it was never standardized.

As soon as a sufficient number of BARs were acquired by the U.S. Marine Corps via transfers from the U.S. Army inventory, the Model of 1941 Johnson Light Machine Gun disappeared from service by 1943. In combat with marines, it had received mixed reviews, with some impressed by the weapon and others feeling it lacked the toughness or reliability necessary for sustained service in the field.

The inventor later submitted for testing to the U.S. Marine Corps Equipment Board an improved version of his light machine gun that he referred to as the Model of 1944 Johnson Light Machine Gun. It had many advanced features over the BAR and was approved by those who tested the weapon. However, that decision was rejected by the senior leadership of the service as it was loath to introduce a new weapon into the inventory by that late stage of the war.

Water-Cooled Machine Guns

Weapons designed by John M. Browning dominated the machine gun segment of the Ordnance Department's inventory during the First and Second World Wars. As he had with the BAR, Browning had anticipated the U.S. Army's need for a water-cooled machine gun at the beginning of the twentieth century and developed one, despite the lack of official U.S. Army interest at the time.

As the American military went to war in April 1917, it took one look at Browning's prototype water-cooled machine gun, firing the .30-06 cartridge, and adopted it as the Browning Machine Gun, Caliber .30, Model of 1917, in May 1917. A total of 70,000 units of the machine gun were built during the First World War. In July 1925, the Ordnance Department dropped the 'Model of' from its weapon designations and it became the Browning Machine Gun, Caliber .30, M1917.

In the 1930s, the Ordnance Department added minor improvements to Browning's original M1917 machine gun design. This upgrading process resulted in the remanu-facturing of almost all the First World War stockpile of the M1917. The upgraded weapon was re-designated the Browning Machine Gun, Caliber .30, M1917A1. During the Second World War the Ordnance Department contracted to have over 50,000 new units of the M1917A1 model constructed to meet wartime demands.

The biggest drawback with the M1917A1 in the opinion of the Ordnance Department, and those delegated to carry them into action, was its weight. The weapon (with water added) weighed in at 41 pounds. Its tripod added another 53.4 pounds.

In addition, the weapon's seven-man crew had to carry the weapon's extra water and ammunition boxes, plus a number of minor accessories.

Due to the combined weight of the M1917A1, including all its various components and accessories, and not the caliber of the weapon, the American military classified it as a 'heavy machine gun'. The role of the heavy machine gun at the infantry battalion level is found in a 1940 War Department manual titled; *Infantry Field Manual: Organization and Tactics of Infantry, The Rifle Battalion*:

> The heavy machine guns execute long-range overhead fires and antiaircraft missions and protect the flanks of advancing rifle units against counterattack. Advancing by echelon, they extend in depth the firepower of the attacking riflemen. They form the most important protective element in the successive bases of fire.

The M1917A1 would be found in the heavy weapons platoon of the infantry company, and in the heavy weapons company of the infantry battalion. Each heavy weapons platoon would have a single heavy machine gun section consisting of two squads, each armed with a M1917A1. The heavy machine gun company of the infantry battalion had two heavy machine gun sections, each armed with two M1917A1s, for a grand total of four M1917A1s.

The individual M1917A1 squad consisted of a squad leader, gunner, assistant gunner, three ammunition carriers, and the driver of the wheeled weapon carrier, referred to as the chauffeur. It was intended that the wheeled weapon carrier would transport the M1917A1 and its squad as close to the frontline as possible. It would then locate and remain in a covered location until such time as the squad leader indicated to the chauffeur it was time to pick them up and move on to the next location.

In the Pacific, the terrain conditions often made it impossible to employ the wheeled weapon carriers assigned to transport the M1917A1 and squad into battle. This often resulted in the weapon being left behind due to the difficulty in hauling it through jungles, or over uneven terrain. A U.S. Marine Corps platoon sergeant, no doubt reflecting on the weight of the M1917A1, commented in a joint U.S. Marine Corps/U.S. Army report titled *Notes on Jungle Warfare* and dated 12 December 1942: 'Put the big rugged men into the heavy weapon company.'

From the same 12 December 1942 comes this comment regarding the employment of the M1917A1 from another marine:

> It pays in the attack in the jungle to use the heavy machine guns. There is a difference of opinion, as you have noticed, on this matter. It is hard work, yes, but don't overlook the value, morale and otherwise, and don't forget about the high rate of fire. If you ditch the heavy machine guns and substitute the lights

[air-cooled] in their place, you must remember that you will be up against the Japanese machine gun.

From a U.S. Army report titled *Battle Experiences Against the Japanese* dated 1 May 1945 appears this extract detailing the extreme measures the Japanese would go to, to locate the position of American machine guns prior to offensive operations:

> The Japanese always try to get [American] machine guns out of action as early as possible. To do this may deliberately expose small groups. Most of these Jap groups can be wiped out with mortars, rifles, carbines or grenades. That keeps the location of the machine guns concealed until the real attack is made ... The Japanese would send men armed with knives and grenades forward to get the machine guns which had repelled the last assault.

Air-Cooled Machine Guns

To address the weight issue with the water-cooled M1917 and M1917A1 machine guns the Ordnance Department began looking into a much lighter air-cooled version of the weapon starting in the 1920s. The eventual result of this line of development appeared in the mid-1930s as the Browning Machine Gun, Caliber .30, M1919A4.

The air-cooled M1919A4 featured a perforated steel jacket for cooling purposes that brought the weapon's weight down to 31 pounds. A newly designed tripod, designated the M2, weighed only 14 pounds. The two-man crew still had to carry the weapon's extra ammunition boxes, plus a number of minor accessories.

The rate of fire of the air-cooled M1919A4 was lower than the water-cooled M1917A1, and could not maintain the sustained firing rate of its water-cooled counterpart. Nor did it have the range of the M1917A1 with its heavier and steadier tripod. These negative features were offset by its lower weight; it was easier to employ alongside the infantrymen it was intended to support in either the offensive or defensive, whereas the heavier water-cooled M1917A1 was often considered un-suitable for any offensive role, and was seen by many as strictly a defensive weapon.

Two M1919A4s were located in the rifle company weapons platoon light machine gun (LMG) section. A description of the role of the light machine gun appears in a 1940 War Department manual titled *Infantry Field Manual: Organization and Tactics of Infantry, the Rifle Battalion:*

> The light machine gun is air-cooled and relatively mobile. Its crew can maintain the march-rate of a rifleman but cannot move at the high speed of the individual rifleman ... Its characteristics fit it for use in the attack for the close support of the smaller infantry units by flanking action: in defense to supplement the action of the heavy machine guns. Within midrange its accuracy is sensibly that of the heavy machine gun.

Only a small number of the air-cooled M1919A4 were built prior to America's official entry into the Second World War. However, once war was declared, American industry built approximately 400,000 units of the M1919A4 during the conflict, with a great many being employed on tanks and other armored fighting vehicles.

A New Version of the Browning .30 Caliber Machine Gun

Even before America's entry into the Second World War, the Ordnance Department was looking for a new light machine to replace the M1919A4 .30 caliber machine gun. However, nothing was developed that offered a significant improvement over the M1919A4. As the Ordnance Department knew that there was no time to develop a new, light, air-cooled machine gun from the ground-up, with war clouds looming over the country, the decision was made to modify the existing M1914A4 design to serve the role.

The new version of the M1919A4 was designated the Browning Machine Gun, M1919A6. It was not standardized by the Ordnance Department, but listed as 'substitute standard', meaning it was only an emergency weapon intended to fill a void in the Ordnance Department inventory until a more suitable weapon could be placed into service.

The M1919A6 featured a new, lighter, perforated steel jacket for cooling purposes, as well as a carrying handle. In place of the M2 tripod used with the M1919A4, the M1919A6 had a detachable shoulder stock and a front-mounted bipod.

With all the weight-saving efforts put into the M1919A6, the Ordnance Department managed to push the weight of the weapon down to a slightly more manageable level than the M1919A4 mounted on its tripod. American industry would produce approximately 40,000 of the M1919A6 with some showing up in service beginning in 1944.

An Overview

A round-up of the general consensus of opinion on the .30 caliber Browning machine guns, be they water-cooled or air-cooled, can be found in a quote found in a March 1945 U.S. Army report: 'The American .30 caliber machine gun is considered one of the best weapons we have. Its rate of fire is sufficient. It is a well-built weapon and very dependable under the toughest conditions.' However, many did complain about the difficulty in changing the weapon's barrel, and its slower rate of fire compared to German machine guns.

First World War Leftover

Prior to the First World War, the Ordnance Department tested and rejected a weapon popularly referred to as the Lewis Light Machine Gun, for use by the U.S. Army. The weapon had been designed by an American inventor, Samuel McClean. In spite of the Ordnance Department's dislike of the weapon, it would be adopted by the British and Belgian Armies and would see widespread employment during the First World War.

Positive impressions by the British and Belgian Armies of the Lewis Light Machine Gun eventually resulted in the U.S. Army purchasing some 350 units of the weapon, chambered for the British .303 cartridge, in 1916. Some of these, as well as others acquired from British Army stockpiles in France, were employed by the American Expeditionary Force (AEF) in 1918. Eventually, the U.S. Army would buy 2,500 units of the weapon, chambered for the American .30-06 cartridge and now standard-ized and designated the Model of 1917 .30 Caliber, Lewis Gun, for stateside training duties only.

The U.S. Marine Corps had embraced the Model of 1917 .30 Caliber, Lewis Gun early on and had the U.S. Navy acquire 6,000 units for them for use in the First World War. However, on arrival in France, the Marines had them taken away and replaced by French weapons, much to the Marines' dismay. Unlike the U.S. Army, which quickly disposed of its Lewis Guns following the First World War, the U.S. Marine Corps would retain the Lewis Gun long enough for it to see action during the Japanese military invasion of the Philippines in December 1941. However, they would all be gone by 1942, replaced by the BAR.

The .50 Caliber Browning Machine Gun

The largest machine gun employed by the American military during the Second World War was a .50 caliber weapon, which came in both water-cooled and air-cooled models. Like the various versions of the .30 caliber machine gun found in the Ordnance Department's inventory in both the First and Second World War, it was designed by John Browning.

The inventor had begun the development of a .50 caliber machine gun during the First World War in response to an Ordnance Department request for a machine gun able to fire a newly developed .50 caliber cartridge. The cartridge was designed by Winchester and resembled a scaled-up version of the standard American military .30-06 cartridge.

The new .50 cartridge was not intended as an anti-personnel round but as an antitank round. There was a perceived threat that late in the First World War the American Expeditionary Force (AEF), fighting in France, would be confronted by large numbers of German tanks, a threat that never materialized. As late as 1940, the weapon was still classified as an antitank weapon in U.S. Army manuals.

Working together with Colt, John Browning came up with a prototype of a .50 caliber machine gun, which was to all effects an enlarged version of his water-cooled .30 caliber machine gun, the M1917. This new .50 caliber machine gun prototype came in a water-cooled format, and an air-cooled version with a perforated steel jacket, intended for mounting on aircraft. Both were tested in November 1918.

The testing of the new prototype .50 caliber machine guns went extremely well, and the Ordnance Department ordered 5,000 of both versions for delivery in 1919. They were to be designated as the Browning .50 caliber Model of M1918. However, with the end of the First World War, the same month as Browning's new .50 caliber gun was ordered, the contract was canceled, and the weapon was never standardized.

Despite the cancelation of his new .50 caliber machine gun, John Browning continued to refine its design. The Ordnance Department assigned the Government-owned and operated Frankford Arsenal the job of improving the ammunition for the weapon, to make it more potent, as the original cartridge design was already being seen as unable to penetrate the armor on the latest tank designs.

Post-First World War testing of the John Browning .50 caliber machine gun and the improved round for the weapon resulted in the Ordnance Department's standardization of it as the water-cooled Browning .50 Caliber, Model of 1921. Despite this adoption of the weapon in 1921, production did not begin until 1926, and then only in very small numbers. By this time, the water-cooled version was seen as both an antitank weapon and antiaircraft weapon.

In 1923, the U.S. Army Air Corps took into service two air-cooled variants of the Model of 1921, with perforated steel jackets. The version intended to be fitted into wings and turrets was referred to as 'fixed', and another hand-operated version for mounting in the fuselages of aircraft as 'flexible'. A slightly improved version of the Model of 1921 was taken into service in 1930, and was assigned the designation 1921A1. In 1933, an upgrade of the Model of 1921A1 appeared and was referred to as the Browning Machine Gun, Caliber .50 M2, Water-Cooled, Flexible.

The Infantry Version of the Browning .50 Caliber Machine Gun

The U.S. Army began thinking about an air-cooled version of the M1921/M1921A1 for mounting in armored fighting vehicles in the 1920s. By the 1930s, the Browning Machine Gun, Heavy Barrel, Caliber .50 M2, HB had appeared, with an air-cooled perforated steel jacket.

For dismounted infantry employment of the new air-cooled variant of the .50 caliber machine gun, the Ordnance Department came up with the Tripod Mount M3. In 1938, the weapon's original 36-inch barrel was replaced with a longer 45-inch barrel to increase the weapon's range and muzzle velocity.

There was one .50 caliber machine gun M2HB authorized for every infantry company heavy weapons platoon, and another for the infantry battalion heavy weapons company. A third .50 caliber machine gun M2HB was assigned to the rifle company headquarters section. At the infantry regimental level there were up to thirty-five additional .50 caliber machine guns M2HB intended for antiaircraft use, or defense of rear area installations.

With armor division armored infantry units their M3 or M3A1 armored halftracks were each armed with a single .50 caliber machine gun M2HB, mainly intended for antiaircraft protection. It was uncommon for the machine gun armed half-tracks to support their onboard infantry squads when disembarked with direct fire, as they were deemed too vulnerable.

On occasion a U.S. Army infantry regiment might combine some of its .50 caliber machine guns M2HB for special assignments, as is demonstrated in this passage from a late-war U.S. Army report titled *Battle Experiences July 1944 to April 1945*:

> A battery of twelve .50 caliber machine guns was organized for one operation by taking guns from the headquarters, service, antitank, and cannon companies. The commanding officer of the heavy weapon company of the reserve battalion [three infantry battalions per infantry regiment] located positions for the guns, assembled the crews, and supervised preparation for the positions for the guns. The battery gave direct support to the battalion making the main effort by neutralizing known enemy positions. This fire was effective and permitted the rapid advance of the leading companies …

The combination of the 84lb .50 caliber machine gun M2HB and its 44lb tripod M3 meant it was not an easy load to move around the battlefield on foot, as with the .30 caliber water-cooled M1917A1 machine guns in the heavy weapon platoon or company in the rifle battalions. The .50 caliber machine guns M2 were normally transported by wheeled weapon carriers that would remain as close to the infantry companies as possible so the weapons could be dismounted quickly when required. The .50 caliber machine guns M2 assigned to the non-infantry units of the infantry regiment were normally mounted on trucks for antiaircraft duties.

(*Opposite above*) A pre-Second World War photograph shows a U.S. Army soldier aiming his Model of 1918 BAR. The weapon weighed 16lbs and was 47 inches in length, which included a removable cylindrical flash hider. It could be fired in semi-automatic or full automatic mode. The 20-round detachable BAR magazine weighed seven ounces when empty and one pound seven ounces when fully loaded. (*NA*)

(*Opposite below*) A Winchester company photograph of the original Model of 1918 Browning Automatic Rifle (BAR). A key spotting feature of this first version of the weapon was the large wooden forearm that encompassed most of the rear portion of the barrel. The wooden forearm featured a checkered pattern etched into a section of it to provide those firing the weapon a better grip. (*NA*)

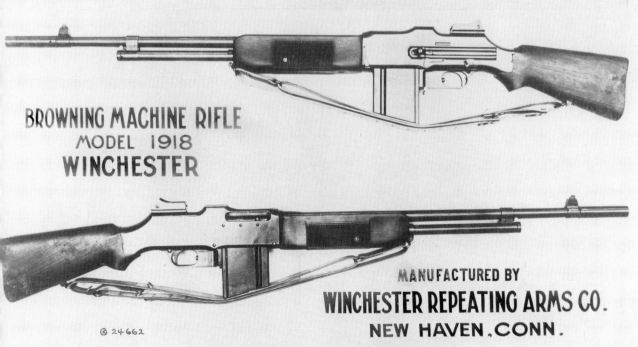

BROWNING MACHINE RIFLE
MODEL 1918
WINCHESTER

MANUFACTURED BY
WINCHESTER REPEATING ARMS CO.
NEW HAVEN, CONN.

Ⓑ 24662

(*Above*) The replacement for the M1918 BAR was designated the Browning Automatic Rifle, Caliber .30, M1918A2 seen here. The original batch consisted of modernized M1918 models, as well as an interim interwar version labeled the M1918A1. Firing from a prone position is a U.S. Army infantryman armed with an M1918A2 BAR fitted with a bipod. (*NA*)

(*Opposite above*) As the supply of pre-Second World War M1918 and M1918A1 BARs was depleted, the Ordnance Department awarded contracts for renewed construction of the M1918A2. Pictured is a new built M1918A2 version of the BAR with tripod. A spotting feature of the new production units was the cut down wooden forearm, which lacked the checkered pattern seen on the forearm of the earlier BARs. (*USMCHC*)

(*Opposite below*) Beside the bipod seen in this picture is a U.S. Army infantryman in a prone firing position with an M1918A2 BAR. Other features that appeared on the weapon included a hinged butt plate, as well as new sights. The addition of the bipod and the hinged butt plate were done to assist the operator in steadying the weapon when firing from a prone or fixed position. (*NA*)

Due to the high rate of fire of the M1918A2 BAR, it was considered a crew-served weapon, as seen here. This meant there was a second man assigned to assist the BAR gunner, referred to in manuals as the 'automatic rifleman'. The 'assistant automatic rifleman' was responsible for maintaining the ammunition supply for the gunner, helping to clear stoppages, identifying targets, or replacing the gunner if he became a casualty. (NA)

Here we see a U.S. Army soldier armed with a modernized M1918 or M1918A1 BAR brought up to the M1918A2 standard. It retains the wooden forearm of the earlier versions of the weapon. The cut-down wooden forearm seen on new M1918A2 BARs was done to increase the cooling of the weapon's barrel, and to prevent charring of the forearm during prolonged firing. (NA)

Due to the various components added to the M1918A2, such as the bipod and hinged butt plate, the weight of the weapon rose to over 20lbs. To cut down on the weight of the 1918A2 BAR, it was not uncommon for soldiers and marines to discard the 2.28lb bipod, as is seen in this picture of a U.S. Army infantryman. (NA)

(*Above left*) A U.S. Army soldier armed with an M1918A2 BAR stands guard on the roof of a house in North Africa. From a Second World War U.S. Army publication titled *Combat Lessons No. 5* appears this quote: 'For a while the Germans thought our BAR was a machine gun, but by the time they brought fire on the BAR it had moved and was firing on them from another direction.' (*NA*)

(*Above right*) A marine takes aim with his M1918A2 BAR. A wartime manual on the weapon states that the BAR gunner, referred to as an automatic rifleman, must be trained to place a large amount of accurate fire upon probable enemy locations and indistinct or concealed targets such as enemy machine guns or small groups of enemy personnel. (*NA*)

(*Opposite above*) A marine is shown firing his M1918A2. A wartime U.S. Marine Corps manual describes the BAR as the most vital weapon of both the infantry squads and platoons. It goes on to state that all men in the squad or platoon must be familiar with the operation and functioning of the BAR in case the automatic rifleman, or the assistant automatic rifleman is killed or wounded. (*NA*)

(*Opposite below*) A marine armed with an M1918A2 BAR awaits the enemy. From a U.S. Army publication titled *Combat Lessons No. 1* appears this extract about its effectiveness in the Pacific: 'The Browning Auto Rifle gave excellent service. This weapon has high jungle mobility and provides excellent firepower for the short-range targets frequently encountered … and to destroy snipers.' (*NA*)

The M1918A2 was not without design flaws, the biggest being the lack of a quick change barrel. This design feature mandated that the BAR gunner closely monitor the number of rounds expended in battle, so his weapon wouldn't overheat. Its Japanese military counterpart, the Type 96 had a quick change barrel, as did the BAR's British military counterpart, known as the Bren gun. (NA)

A U.S. Army infantryman armed with an M1918A2 BAR is shown escorting two German prisoners of war into captivity. Unlike the M1918 and the M1918A1 BARs, the M1918A2 was only capable of full-automatic fire. The weapon's effective rate of fire was 120–150 rounds per minute, with a sustained rate of 40–60 rounds per minute. (NA)

A marine armed with an M1928A2 BAR fires on the enemy. He appears to be steadying the weapon with an unseen pistol grip under the forearm, a feature that appeared late in the Pacific campaigns. The effective rate of fire of the BAR depended on the dexterity of the gunner in changing magazines. Maximum effective range of the weapon was approximately 500 yards. (NA)

A U.S. Army infantryman armed with his M1918A2 BAR covers a surrendering German soldier. An experienced BAR gunner could (with trigger manipulation) fire two to three round bursts, or four to five round bursts. It was up to the BAR gunner to fire his weapon in bursts and at the rate of fire that would be the most effective for the existing conditions. (NA)

A marine armed with an M1918A2 BAR warily scans his surroundings for any sign of enemy activity. Another design fault with the BAR series was the under-the-receiver 20-round detachable box magazine, which severely limited its ability to deliver sustained fire on the battlefield. Its Japanese counterpart, the Type 96, fed from a curved 30-round magazine that was inserted into the top of the weapon's receiver. (NA)

A marine armed with an M1918A2 BAR engages the enemy, while the assistant automatic rifleman is shown pulling the pin on a hand grenade. From a publication titled *Combat Lessons No. 2* is this extract on the BAR: 'The Browning Automatic Rifle was found to be invaluable in the attack because of its mobility and firepower, and patrols were always reinforced with automatic rifle teams.' (NA)

A marine is shown armed with the Model of 1941 Johnson Light Machine Gun. It weighed approximately 13 pounds and had an overall length of 42 inches. It fired from a 20-round detachable box magazine that was inserted into the right hand side of the receiver. Rejected by the U.S. Army, it was taken into service by the U.S. Marine Corps in very small numbers. (NA)

The Browning Machine Gun, Caliber .30, M1917A1 seen here was a modernized version of the original Browning Machine Gun, Caliber .30, M1917, introduced into service during the First World War. America's entry into the Second World War resulted in the building of new units of the M1917A1 machine gun because the original First World War inventory of the weapon was quickly exhausted. (NA)

The M1917A1 .30 caliber machine gun was a liquid-cooled weapon, as is evidenced by the water jacket that surrounds the barrel of this M1917A1 being pointed skyward by a U.S. Army soldier. The weapon's cyclic rate of fire was listed as 450–650 rounds per minute. (NA)

Historical re-enactors in early Second World War U.S. Marine Corps uniforms are shown with a Lewis Gun in the foreground, and an M1903 Springfield rife in the background. Both weapons had seen use in the First World War and had remained in the American military arsenal long enough to see combat in the next world-wide conflict. (*USMCHC*)

In this picture, we see a historical re-enactor in a U.S. Marine Corps uniform from the Second World War taking aim with a version of the standard M1903 Springfield rife modified into a sniper rifle. It was fitted with an 8 × Unertl scope that was marked as 'U.S.M.C. Sniper'. (*USMCHC*)

The historical re-enactors seen in this picture wear one of the various types of camouflage uniforms issued during the Second World War. They are armed with the Rifle, Caliber .30 M1. It was the replacement for the M1903 Springfield rife in the U.S. Army before America's official entry into the Second World War, and the U.S. Marine Corps during the conflict.

A historical re-enactor appears in this picture wearing a U.S. Army Second World War uniform, as issued to airborne troops. In addition, he is shown with a military police marked helmet and armband. He is armed with a weapon officially designated the Carbine, Caliber .30 M1. It is best known today as the 'M1 carbine' and was the most widely produced American small arm of the Second World War.

(Michael Green)

Dressed in historical copies of U.S. Marine Corps uniforms from the Second World War are two re-enactors posing with a Browning Machine Gun, Caliber .30, M1917A1. The original model of the water-cooled machine gun was labeled the M1917 and saw action with the American military in the First World War. The M1917A1 was listed as a 'heavy machine gun' due to the weapon's weight. (USMCHC)

As a lighter alternative to the Browning Machine Gun, Caliber .30, M1917A1 for infantry units, the Ordnance Department came up with the much lighter air-cooled Browning Machine Gun, Caliber .30 M1919A4. An example is seen here with all the various supporting components and accessories the weapon's two-man crew brought into battle with them. (USMCHC)

A re-enactor dressing in the uniform of a Second World War Marine is shown with an M1 Carbine, a weapon that the USMC used to replace various submachine guns. American military re-enactors perform a valuable service in presenting to the public both the uniforms and weapons employed by those who served during the last World War. (*DOD*)

In a well-protected defensive emplacement is seen the two man U.S. Army crew of a 60mm Mortar M2. The small weapon weighed with mount a total of 42lbs, with the mortar tube being only 28.6-inches long. It could fire a 2.94lb high-explosive shell labeled the M49A2, or a 3.72lb illuminating shell designated the M83, employed to disclose targets at night. (*NA*)

Among the many weapons employed by the American military during the Second World War was a series of different flamethrowers. The final model was referred to as the M2-2, with two being seen in use during a training exercise. The two flamethrower operators are shown covered by three BAR equipped soldiers. (NA)

Shown is an example of the Browning Automatic Rifle, Caliber .30, M1918A2, best known during the Second World War and today as the 'BAR'. When issued, it was fitted with a bipod, however, that feature was typically removed to save weight. The carrying handle on the BAR began appearing on the weapon in December 1944.

Standing in the doorway of a C-47 transport plane in this posed photograph is a U.S. Army paratrooper. His M1 Rifle has been broken down into its various components and stored inside the rectangular canvas pouch on the front of his chest. On his shoulder is an M1A1 2.36-inch Antitank Rocket Launcher, better known to all by its popular nickname, the 'Bazooka'. (NA)

U.S. Army soldiers are shown posed for the Signal Corps photographer as if they are ready to commence firing with their 57mm Gun M1. The weapon was British-designed but built under license in the United States during the Second World War to equip U.S. Army and U.S. Marine Corps infantry divisions. The American-built version differed in some minor ways from its British counterpart. *(NA)*

Belonging to a private collector in the United States is this non-operational example of the 105mm Howitzer M2A1. Ammunition for the weapon was of the semi-fixed type, which meant the projectile could be removed from the cartridge case for adjustment of the charge zone. The more charges inserted into the cartridge case before it was joined together with the projectile dictated its range. *(Michael Green)*

The U.S. Army 105mm Howitzer M3 shown here was a lightweight and smaller version of the standard 105mm Howitzer M2A1. It fired the same ammunition as its larger cousin, but the cartridge cases contained smaller propelling charges to achieve the desired rapid combustion needed due to the weapon's shorter barrel. (*NA*)

The half-track personnel carrier M3A1 shown here was 8 feet 10 inches tall with the pulpit-mounted .50 caliber machine gun fitted. The vehicle had authorized storage for 700 rounds of .50 caliber ammunition and 7,750 rounds of .30 caliber machine gun ammunition. In addition, it could carry 24 M1A1 antitank mines. (*Bob Fleming*)

In this photograph of two marines manning a .30 caliber M1917A1 machine gun can be seen the water condensing can and the hose that connected it to the water jacket. Liquid circulating between the weapon's water jacket and condensing can allowed the machine gun a sustained rate of fire of 125 rounds per minute. (NA)

The water condensing can, which was one of the numerous accessories that had to be lugged around with the M1917A1 .30 caliber machine gun, was intended to prevent steam from being generated by the evaporation of water on a heated barrel giving away the position of the weapon and crew in battle, as is seen in this picture. (NA)

(*Above*) The M1917A1 .30 caliber machine gun receiver was fed by a woven fabric belt with a capacity of 250 rounds. The only metal employed in the belt was a brass tab at either end to facilitate entering the belt into the weapon's left hand side feed slot, as seen in this picture. A disintegrating metallic ammunition belt was developed for the aircraft-mounted version of the weapon. (*NA*)

(*Opposite above*) Here an ice-encrusted M1917A1 .30 caliber machine gun and crew. The weapon itself (with water) weighed approximately 41lbs. The tripod that supported it weighed approximately 52lbs, for a grand total of 93lbs. The American military therefore classified the M1971A1 as a 'heavy machine gun'. (*NA*)

(*Opposite below*) The tripod that supported the M1917A1 .30 caliber machine gun, seen here on the back of one of the weapon's crew, was designated as the M1917A1 tripod. It consisted of two major components, as seen in this picture. The bottom portion was made up of a three-leg arrangement upon which the upper cradle assembly sat. The cradle held the weapon in place and allowed it to be traversed and elevated. (*NA*)

(*Above*) A snow-covered M1917A1 .30 caliber machine gun and crew is shown here. According to a 1942 U.S. Army manual, the weapon's tripod mount allowed it to deliver accurate overhead fire and allowed for firing at night from predetermined data. The actual range of the M1917A1 employing direct fire was often limited by observation, which was rarely effective beyond 2,000 yards. (*NA*)

(*Opposite above*) Set up in a multi-story building is a U.S. Army M1917A1 .30 caliber machine gun and crew. In wartime manuals, the primary target for the weapon was exposed enemy personnel, especially if they were in close formation, or in depth with respect to the line of fire. Secondary targets would be entrenched enemy personnel, observation posts, opposing machine guns, and antitank guns. (*NA*)

(*Opposite below*) U.S. Army soldiers are shown in a defensive position guarding a portable bridge. U.S. Army manuals from the time state that heavy machine guns such as the M1917A1 .30 caliber machine gun should be assigned to long-range targets, especially those too close to the attacking friendly infantry to be dealt with by artillery or mortar fire. (*NA*)

(*Above*) A wartime quote by the 3rd Marine Regiment fighting on the island of Bougainville: 'There was no opportunity to use machine guns in distant support or to deliver fire by overhead or indirect fire methods. Direct support machine guns had to be right in the front lines.' Evidence for this is seen in this picture of marines manning an M1917A1 .30 caliber machine gun in dense jungle undergrowth. (*NA*)

(*Opposite above*) Pictured are marines lugging an M1917A1 .30 caliber machine gun and accessories up a steep cliff face. The weapon's weight was an ongoing problem. A wartime report written following the Bougainville Campaign mentions the issue: 'Light automatic and semi-automatic weapons (Thompson Sub-Machine Gun, BAR, and M1 rifle) delivered the bulk of the offensive firepower and were more used than ground-mount machine guns because of their lightness and greater flexibility.' (*NA*)

(*Opposite below*) A U.S. Army infantryman armed with an M1917A1 .30 caliber machine gun watches for any sign of enemy activity to his front. For close-in protection he has two fragmentation hand grenades nearby. U.S. Army manuals of the period stress that whenever practicable the M1917A1 be fired from emplacements. (*NA*)

(*Above*) The U.S. Army crew of an M1917A1 .30 caliber machine gun has taken up a defensive position in a building. It was pointed out to machine gun crews that the enemy regarded them as important targets in battle, and would always be looking for the distinctive noise of their weapon firing, as well as the muzzle blast of the weapon. (*NA*)

(*Opposite above*) A U.S. Army M1917A1 .30 caliber machine gun crew is shown moving forward with their weapon and its accessories. Whenever possible, the M1917A1 and crew were to be transported as close to their intended location as possible by a weapons carrier. Once on foot, the M1917A1 crew would have the same mobility as riflemen for only a short period of time. (*NA*)

(*Opposite below*) The Ordnance Department was not unaware of the difficulty of moving the M1917A1 .30 caliber machine gun once it was removed from its wheeled weapon carrier, especially in rugged terrain. For these situations, a number of small hand carts were placed into service during the Second World War. Here we see an example restored by a private collector. (*Michael Green*)

(*Above*) A marine M1917A1 .30 caliber machine gun is shown laying down sustained suppressive fire. The 250-round fabric belt that was fed into the receiver of the weapon typically had 1 tracer round to 4 ball rounds or 1 tracer round to every 4 armor-piercing rounds. The 250-round ammunition containers seen in the picture were made of stamped steel. (*NA*)

(*Opposite above*) Firing from within the ruin of a building is a gunner on a 1917A1 .30 caliber machine gun. When battlefield conditions dictated, the M1917A1 could perform rapid fire, which was 250 rounds per minute. This rate of fire could be maintained for several minutes, but the barrel would overheat and generate steam that would give away the weapon's position. (*NA*)

(*Opposite below*) The American fighting man was not averse to employing captured enemy weapons if a sufficient amount of ammunition was available. Here we see a marine posing with a captured Japanese type, Heavy Machine Gun that fired a 7.7mm round. It was an air-cooled weapon, as is evidenced by the cooling fins running down the length of the barrel. (*NA*)

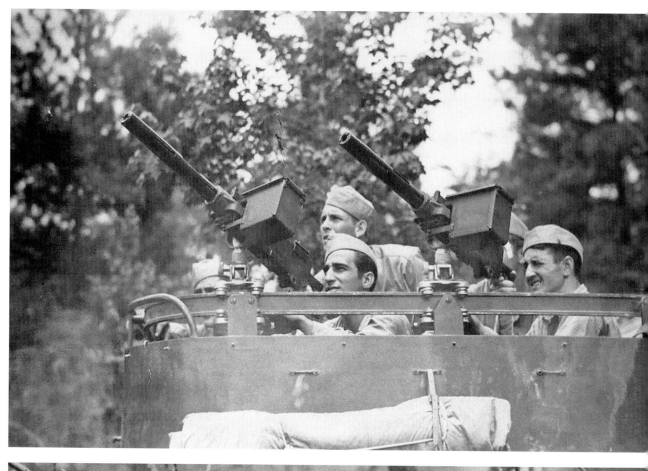

(*Opposite above*) In 1919, the Ordnance Department took into service an air-cooled version of the M1917A1 .30 caliber machine gun for use on tanks, labeled the M1919. In the 1920s, it was modified to become an infantry machine gun referred to as the M1919A1. Two examples of a version for the Cavalry Branch of the U.S. Army labeled the M1919A2 are shown vehicle-mounted during a pre-Second World War training exercise. (*NA*)

(*Opposite below*) The M1919A1 and M1919A2 machine guns were fitted with 18-inch barrels. Their replacement was an improved version, intended for infantry use, referred to as the M1919A3. It was fitted with a 24-inch barrel. An updated model labeled the M1919A4 was the variant that saw use in the Second World War. An example is seen here mounted on its M2 tripod. (*NA*)

(*Above*) Two marines are shown with their M1919A4 .30 caliber machine gun. It was officially designated by the Ordnance Department as the Browning Machine Gun, Caliber .30, M1919A4. The weapon weighed 31lbs, and the tripod about 19lbs, for a combined weight of approximately 50lbs. It was classified by the American military as a 'light machine gun' and was primarily seen as an offensive weapon. (*NA*)

(*Above*) American military personnel have built an elaborate emplacement for their M1919A4 .30 caliber machine gun, including overhead cover from the sun. While the maximum rate of fire for the weapon was 400–500 rounds per minute for short periods of time, the weapon's normal rate of fire was 150 rounds per minute. (*NA*)

(*Opposite above*) Marines in the Pacific are shown engaged in a firefight with a variety of weapons. In the foreground is a marine armed with the 1918A2 BAR, while the marine in the background is firing a tripod-mounted M1919A4 .30 caliber machine gun. The M2 tripod was portable, easily packed, and intended to provide a steady mount for accurate fire on ground targets. (*NA*)

(*Opposite below*) The M2 Tripod for the M1919A4 .30 caliber machine gun consisted of three tubular steel legs which met at the tripod head. The two trail legs were joined and additionally supported by a traversing bar, seen here forming a simple A-truss that served as the rear support for the gun when mounted. (*NA*)

(*Above*) A U.S. Army infantryman is shown carrying an M1919A4 .30 caliber machine gun into battle. When an infantry rifle company organized a base of fire, its two-gun light machine gun section would be assigned a target or targets, or a fire section. Directing the fire of the machine gun section fell to the section leader. (*NA*)

(*Opposite above*) Two marines man an M1919A4 .30 caliber machine gun. Unlike the M1917A1 .30 caliber machine gun, which was suitable for both direct and indirect fire at long ranges in a sustained mode the M1919A4 was considered strictly a direct fire weapon intended to deliver fire at close and midrange targets in short bursts. (*NA*)

(*Opposite below*) The crew of an M1919A4 .30 caliber machine gun watches for any signs of enemy activity. Prior to being assigned firing positions, it was the job of the section leader to go ahead of his two machine gun crews to note the location of friendly frontline troops and find the best location for deploying his weapons. Also important was identifying actual or suspected hostile machine gun positions. (*NA*)

(*Above*) A young marine takes aim with his M1919A4 .30 caliber machine gun. When positions were chosen by the section leader of a machine gun section it was always stressed in training and in the manuals that the two machine gun positions be separated by a certain distance to protect against both guns being destroyed by the same artillery burst. (*NA*)

(*Opposite above*) Two U.S. Army infantrymen take cover along a stone fence with their M1919A4 .30 caliber machine gun. It was the responsibility of the two-gun light machine section leader to constantly seek out new firing positions for his weapons to maximize their effectiveness in combat. Overseeing the section leader would be the weapon platoon or company commander. (*NA*)

(*Opposite below*) In this unusual image, we see an M1919A4 .30 caliber machine gun mounted on the M1917A1 tripod for the M1917A1 .30 caliber machine gun. Battlefield firing positions for the two-gun light machine gun section in the infantry company was typically within hailing or arm-and-hand signal distance of each other for better control by the section leader. (*NA*)

Shown walking gingerly over a wooden ladder over a swollen creek is a U.S. Army infantryman with an M1919A4 .30 caliber machine gun slung over his shoulder. When engaging the enemy in battle, it was the section leader of a two-machine gun section that normally designated targets, specified the number of rounds to be fired, and gave the signal to open fire. (NA)

An exhausted looking pair of marines, making up the two-man team of an M1919A4 .30 caliber machine gun, is shown taking a break during the fighting to catch their breath and a cigarette. When an infantry company advanced into the attack, the machine gun section typically marched alongside a flank, and would occupy a successive number of firing positions to be ready to lend fire support when called upon. (NA)

Shown in a defensive emplacement is a U.S. Army soldier armed with an M1919A4 .30 caliber machine gun. Visible in this photo is the aluminum pistol-type handgrip for the weapon. Also seen projecting downwards underneath the rear of the weapon's receiver is the traversing and elevating mechanism. The number of M191A4s was always higher within infantry divisions than the M1917A1. (NA)

German prisoners of war are shown being transported into captivity aboard a jeep. Behind them in the rear of the vehicle is a grim-faced American soldier armed with an M3 submachine gun. The jeep is armed on the passenger side with an M1919A4 .30 caliber machine gun fitted onto the M1917A1 tripod cradle, which in turn is mounted on either an M24 or M24C pedestal mount. (NA)

In what appears to be a field experiment to make the M1919A4 .30 caliber machine gun lighter for improved battlefield mobility, the weapon's tripod has been done away with and in its place the M1919A4 has been fitted with an improvised bipod, attached to the perforated barrel support jacket with a very short section of rope. It also features a makeshift carrying handle just above the mid-point of the gun. (NA)

Pictured is the Ordnance Department's official lightened variant of the M1919A4 .30 caliber machine gun, officially designated the Browning Machine Gun, Caliber .30, 1919A6. The key weight-saving item was a new thinner and lighter barrel. It also featured a number of removable components, as seen in this picture, such as the butt stock, carrying handle, and an M1918A2 BAR based bipod. (NA)

Shown is a U.S. Army Browning Machine Gun, Caliber .30, 1919A6, mounted on the standard M1919A4 tripod designated the M2. The key spotting feature of the 1919A6 was the new muzzle (recoil) booster at the very end of the barrel, which differed from the shape of the muzzle booster on the M1919A4. The crew has removed the butt stock and carrying handle. (NA)

Two U.S. Army infantrymen are shown firing their M1919A6 .30 caliber machine gun. The weapon's removable butt stock weighed 1.75lbs and was made of stamped metal. The carrying handle was made of plastic. Notice the improvised leather sling attached around the mid-point of the perforated barrel jacket back to the butt stock. (NA)

Another First World War era weapon that survived in service long enough with the U.S. Marine Corps to see employment at the very beginning of the war, following the Japanese attack on Pearl Harbor, was the air-cooled Lewis Light Machine Gun. Here we see a picture of two First World War American soldiers firing the weapon from an improvised antiaircraft mount. (NA)

A U.S. Marine Corps motorcycle dispatch rider is seen here in a no doubt posed photograph taking a nap while clutching his Lewis Light Machine Gun. Rather than a pillow, he rests his head on a 47-round pan magazine that was mounted on the top of the receiver. By the end of 1942, the last of the Lewis Guns had been replaced in U.S. Marine Corps service by various versions of the BAR. (NA)

A marine mans a Browning Machine Gun, Caliber .30, M2, Water-Cooled, Flexible. It is emplaced as an antiaircraft weapon. In the U.S. Army the weapon was a non-divisional asset, but in the U.S. Marine Corps wartime infantry divisions of 1942, it was a divisional asset. The weapon weighed 100.5lbs without water jacket. (NA)

Visible in this training photo prior to America's entry into the Second World War is a Browning Machine Gun, Heavy Barrel, Caliber .50, M2HB, mounted on the M3 ground tripod. The weapon pictured is an early production unit, as it had a 36-inch barrel and slots rather than holes in its perforated barrel support jacket, as appeared on later production units. (NA)

The 100-round ammunition belt visible in this training photograph being fed into an early production unit of the .50 caliber machine gun M2HB, was made of fabric with metal tips. It proved unpopular because the weapon's feed tray mechanism was not strong enough to support its weight, which resulted in jamming. (NA)

Here we see an early production .50 caliber machine gun M2HB being employed in the antiaircraft role. It is mounted on a pedestal, with a crewmember physically supporting the weight of the fabric ammunition belt as it feeds into the weapon's receiver. To correct the problem of the fabric ammunition belts jamming the weapon's feed tray mechanism, it was eventually redesigned with stronger belt feed paws. (NA)

The gunner on this early production .50 caliber machine gun M2HB looks through the M1 telescopic sight, which was a removable accessory for the weapon. It was seldom employed during the Second World War, based on pictorial evidence. Wartime pictorial evidence shows that the early production perforated barrel support jacket, with holes instead of slots, remained in use until the end of the Second World War. (NA)

(*Above*) Eventually, the fabric ammunition belts for the .50 caliber machine gun M2HB were replaced with 100-round disintegrating metallic link belts, as seen here in use by these marines. The M3 ground mount tripod for the .50 caliber machine gun M2HB shown here was adopted in 1933. With its three legs fully extended, the weapon was only 13-inches off the ground. (*NA*)

(*Opposite above*) Shown is a late production .50 caliber machine gun M2HB, with a 45-inch barrel, and a perforated barrel jacket featuring holes for cooling purposes, rather than slots, as seen on the early production units of the weapon. The longer barrel for the weapon was introduced in 1937 which improved muzzle velocity and provided increased range. (*NA*)

(*Opposite below*) The U.S. Army crew of a .50 caliber machine gun M2HB enters a destroyed German building to look for a suitable firing position. Two men carry the gun itself, and the third man carries the M3 ground tripod. The German military had nothing comparable to the weapon and greatly feared its use when employed in a ground support role against them. (*NA*)

(*Above*) Manning a .50 caliber machine gun M2HB is a single U.S. Army soldier. The weapon had an adjustable leaf sight on the rear of the receiver that was graduated 100–2,500 yards. On the front of the receiver was a hooded blade sight, as seen in this picture. When firing no more than 40 rounds per minute in bursts of 5–7 rounds, the fire of the weapon could be sustained almost indefinitely. (*NA*)

(*Opposite above*) The U.S. Army crew of a .50 caliber machine gun M2HB appears to be in the process of adjusting the weapon's rear leaf sight. The American military had no illusions about the ability of a single .50 caliber machine gun M2HB to shoot down low-flying planes. However, they felt that the tracer fire of the weapon in close proximity to an attacking aircraft would have a deterrent effect on enemy pilots. (*NA*)

(*Opposite below*) The crew of a .50 caliber machine gun M2HB are shown posing as if engaging an aerial threat. The weapon is fitted on a pedestal mounted in the rear cargo bay of a ³⁄₄-ton truck. The principal classes of ammunition for the .50 caliber machine gun M2 were, and remain today: ball, armor-piercing, incendiary, armor-piercing incendiary, and tracer. (*NA*)

From a jeep, a U.S. Army soldier fires his pedestal-mounted .50 caliber machine gun M2HB as a second soldier observes the fall of the shot with a pair of binoculars. The 100-round ammunition belts for the weapon were typically belted in the ratio of 2 armor-piercing, 2 incendiary, and 1 tracer round. Tracer rounds would burn out somewhere between 1,850 and 2,450 yards. *(NA)*

A photograph of a field-improvised towed gun carriage for .50 caliber machine gun M2HB fitted with armor shield. Unlike any of the .30 caliber Browning machine guns employed by the American military during the Second World War, the .50 caliber machine gun M2 had the ability to fire semi-automatic and full automatic. *(NA)*

Members of a U.S. Army crew of an M3A1 halftrack in England are preparing their vehicle for the upcoming invasion of France in June 1944. Very visible is the vehicle's .50 caliber machine gun M2HB mounted in an armored pulpit over the passenger seat. A total of 374,524 units of the weapon were built during the Second World War. (NA)

An armored infantry squad is shown having disembarked from their M3A1 armored half-track. The vehicle appears to be mounted with two .50 caliber machine gun M2HBs. In theory, every U.S. Army mechanized infantry battalion in 1943 was supposed to have only forty-three of the .50 caliber machine gun M2HB. In the field, it was not uncommon for such units to acquire many more weapons than officially authorized. *(NA)*

Chapter Three

Infantry Support Weapons

It was clear to armies around the world that the introduction of the tank during the First World War would require that infantrymen be provided with antitank weapons. However, as the American military shrank in size following the conflict, and its budget constricted, the development of a suitable antitank gun for the infantry branch was not a high priority.

The only weapon in the U.S. Army inventory during the 1920s through the early 1930s that could have been considered an antitank weapon was a small, towed, French-designed 37mm gun adopted during the First World War and assigned the designation 37mm Gun, M1916. The U.S. Army acquired most from the French Army during the conflict, but also ordered a large number of American-built copies, of which only a very few saw combat.

Of the 2,598 units of the 37mm Gun, M1916 ordered from American firms during the First World War, only 884 would enter U.S. Army service before the contract was canceled when the conflict came to an end. Due to its short range and low velocity, it was clear by the early 1930s that the towed 37mm Gun, M1916 was obsolete as an antitank weapon, and the search began for its replacement. What was eventually selected was a modified version of a towed German 37mm antitank gun.

A New Antitank Gun for the Infantry

The modified license-built copy of the towed German 37mm antitank gun was adopted in 1938 by the Ordnance Department and was originally designated the 37mm Gun M3, with the first examples delivered to the U.S. Army in 1940. There were eighteen authorized per U.S. Army infantry battalion in the 1940 TO&E.

Shortly after the introduction of the 37mm Gun M3 into service, production began of another version labeled the 37mm Gun M3A1 that had its muzzle threaded for the mounting of a muzzle brake, which was never fitted, as the weapon could no longer fire its canister round.

The desire of the Infantry Branch of the U.S. Army to take the new towed 37mm Gun M3 into service was questioned by some in the Ordnance Department who were aware that it lacked the range and ability to penetrate the armor on many existing tanks. This view can be seen in a quote by the Chief of the U.S. Army Artillery

Branch of the Manufacturing Division from 1937 to 1939 prior to America's official entry into the Second World War:

> The Ordnance Department was well aware that the 37mm gun was totally inadequate as an antitank gun, and many repeated efforts were made to convince the various interested service personnel of the fact. It is my opinion that all of the early artillery of World War II … suffered from the continued insistence by the using arms on mobility, even at the expense of striking power.

Into Combat

In spite of such comments, the 37mm Gun M3 went to war with the U.S. Army infantrymen assigned to Operation Torch, the American military invasion of French North Africa in November 1942. Eventually, when the U.S. Army encountered the tanks of the German Afrika Corps in February 1943, the shortcomings of the weapon were exposed. This is illustrated in this passage from a U.S. Army report titled *Training Notes from Recent Fighting in Tunisia* concerning the combat action that took place in March 1943:

> There has been considerable variation in experience with the 37mm antitank gun … all agree that the 37mm is effective only when properly employed with full understanding of its potentialities and limitations … In our first experience, attempts were made to engage tanks at long range, 1,000 yards or more. The gunners would get excited and open fire at such ranges and thus give away their position. The tanks with heavier caliber guns would outrange and knock out the 37s. Our experiences taught us after we had paid in casualties that the 37mm with the new ammunition (M51) is effective at ranges of 300–375 yards … The best positions are defilade on flanks, so as to reach the target on its flanks or rear.

Combat experience gained in North Africa in the spring of 1943 led to replacement of the 37mm M3 in the majority of U.S. Army infantry units by other antitank weapons. However, in the Pacific, the 37mm Gun M3 was much more effective against the occasional encounter with Japanese tanks. It would serve until the end of the Second World War in that theater. Rather, then armor piercing rounds, the most commonly used rounds were either high-explosive or canister rounds.

The pre-war emphasis on light weight for the 37mm Gun M3 by the U.S. Army infantry branch worked to its advantage in the Pacific on occasion as seen in this extract from a 1 May 1945 U.S. Army report titled *Battle Experiences Against the Japanese*:

> The 37mm gun is admittedly a weapon of opportunity in the jungle. Once we disassembled a 37mm gun and carried it through heavy foliage. We assembled it

under cover, moved it rapidly into the open and destroyed a Jap field piece and killed its crew. Once we used canister effectively against [Japanese] assault boats.

A New Antitank Gun

In early 1941, the Ordnance Department began a project aimed at having a British designed and built towed antitank gun referred to then as the 'Six-Pounder', built in the United States for Lend Lease purposes. This was done to take the pressure off already seriously overburdened British industry. At the time, the British military labeled its antitank guns and artillery pieces not by their bore diameter, as did the American military, but rather by the weight of the typical armor-piercing round fired.

British liaison officers, based in the United States, suggested to those in the Ordnance Department, what they already knew, that they considered the 37mm Gun M3 obsolete, and that they should think about replacing it with the Six-Pounder. The Ordnance Department might have concurred with the British opinion on the shortcomings of the 37mm Gun M3, but they had no user requirement for the weapon at that time. However, in anticipation of a possible future requirement, an improved American-built version of the Six-Pounder was adopted as substitute standard in late 1941 as the 57mm Gun, M1.

With the failure of the 37mm Gun M3 in combat in North Africa, the Infantry Branch of the U.S. Army decided to overlook their preoccupation with mobility and adopt the larger and heavier towed 57mm antitank in the spring of 1943. It would become part of the TO&E of U.S. Army infantry divisions in May 1943, and subsequently be taken into service by the U.S. Marine Corps. There were fifty-four of the 57mm antitank guns divided between the three infantry regiments of a U.S. Army infantry division.

Sadly, the 57mm antitank gun proved obsolete by the time it entered service with the U.S. Army infantry divisions. The German military had already placed into service a new generation of more heavily armored tanks and self-propelled guns that were impervious on their frontal armor array against the armor-piercing projectiles (AP) of the 57mm antitank gun.

The only redeeming feature of the 57mm antitank gun during the bulk of the fighting in Europe was the infrequent appearance of large numbers of German tanks and self-propelled guns, except for a few occasions, such as the Battle of the Bulge. Its lack of effectiveness was clear to many in the infantry early on in Europe and they were sometimes left behind in rear area depots rather than being taken into combat, and their crews assigned other jobs. In the Pacific, the 57mm antitank gun, like the 37mm Gun M3, proved useful in a variety of non-antitank roles, as the threat from Japanese tanks was minimal.

An Antitank Rocket Launcher

A novel type of weapon that appeared in the American military inventory during the Second World War was the antitank rocket launcher, better known to most soldiers by its popular nickname as the 'bazooka'. The term bazooka came from the resemblance it had to a strange-looking musical instrument invented by Bob Burns, a well-known American radio comedian of the day. The new weapon would eventually be accepted as being a more effective antitank weapon than either the towed 37mm or 57mm guns in many situations.

The bazooka was invented by Leslie A. Skinner of the Ordnance Department in early 1942. Skinner's invention so impressed those who saw it that it was quickly standardized in June 1942 as the Launcher, Rocket AT (Antitank) M1. The 2.36-inch rocket fired from the M1 Bazooka was designated the M6, and had a shaped charge warhead. General Electric was contracted by the Ordnance Department to build the new antitank weapon.

In the TO&E of any U.S. Army infantry division there were typically 29 bazookas at the infantry battalion level and 112 at the infantry regimental level. In the U.S. Marine Corps infantry divisional structure, the number of authorized bazookas went from a low of 132 in 1942 up to a high of 243 in 1943.

First Combat

Rushed into production, the M1 Bazooka was supplied at the last minute to the U.S. Army troops taking part in the American invasion of French North Africa in November 1942. Sadly, as the soldiers had no time to become familiar with the new weapon, they had little confidence in it. On the evening before the troops boarded the troop ships that were to take them to North Africa, General Dwight Eisenhower, commander of the invasion forces, was shocked when one of his troop commanders told him that he was completely at a loss 'as to how to teach his men the use of the vitally needed weapon'. He went on to say, 'I don't know anything about it myself except from hearsay.'

Needless to say, the M1 Bazooka was off to an unfortunate start in its military career. A number of design issues cropped up during the fighting in North Africa, most being related to the weapon's batteries and the unreliable M6 rocket. There were so many reports of malfunctions that the War Department suspended further issue of the weapon in May 1943. A high-ranking U.S. Army general who visited the North African Theater on the conclusion of the fighting in May 1943 could not find anyone who could say that a tank had been stopped by the M1 Bazooka.

New Model Bazookas

During the American invasion of Sicily in July 1943, the M1 Bazooka with the M6 rocket was given another chance at proving itself in combat. The Ordnance

Department had hoped to deploy an improved model of the M1 Bazooka and M6 Rocket, respectively labeled the M1A1 Bazooka and M6A1 Rocket, for the invasion, but it did not reach the area in time. Instead, the newest version of the bazooka would be saved for the planned invasion of France in mid-1944.

In late 1943, the Ordnance Department, at the request of the U.S. Army Airborne Command, developed a new version of the bazooka designated the Launcher, Rocket, Antitank, 2.36 Inch, M9 that was quickly replaced by the improved M9A1 model. Unlike the long and cumbersome one-piece launcher tube of the earlier model bazookas, the launcher tubes of the M9/M9A1 could be broken down into two separate parts for ease of transport. The Ordnance Department also improved the design of the M6A1 Rocket and came up with a more reliable version designated the M6A3 Rocket.

Some Success at Last

During the fighting in Sicily the M1 Bazooka was credited with four German medium tanks and one Tiger E heavy tank, with a lucky shot through the driver's direct vision visor. But most American soldiers preferred the M9A1 Rifle Grenade when dealing with enemy armored fighting vehicles during the fighting in Sicily.

The main redeeming feature of the M1 Bazooka that won over the American soldiers fighting in Sicily and other locations was its effectiveness against enemy defensive positions. The M1 Bazooka was now thought of as more than just an antitank weapon and was soon in demand. This can be seen in a U.S. Army report dated May 1, 1945 and titled *Battle Experiences Against the Japanese*:

> Opinion as to the value of the bazooka against the Jap pillbox differed. Apparently, the difference depended upon whether units were attacking old or new bunkers. On old bunkers, well covered with vegetation, the attackers often could not see the firing slits until they were so close that a hand grenade could be easily thrown in. On the other hand, slits of some of the new bunkers could be seen as far away as 25 yards. From that distance a good bazooka operator could place a rocket through a slit or right beside it. One unit which favored the bazooka knocked out twelve bunkers with it in one day.

From a U.S. Army report covering the period from July 1944 to April 1945 titled *Battle Experiences* appears this extract on how to make the most efficient use of the bazooka in the European Theater of Operation:

a. Select aggressive men.
b. Make the bazooka their primary weapon. Give them only a pistol in addition.
c. Put bazooka teams for training and operation under a noncommissioned officer who has used a bazooka in battle and believes in it.

d. Give bazooka personnel special training to include the following:
      (1) Vulnerable points on hostile tanks.
      (2) Emplacing the bazooka to obtain concealment and surprise.
      (3) Tank stalking. This should be by patrols of two bazooka teams and a rifle squad with several submachine guns.
      (4) Use your bazooka in pairs under company control unless a special situation makes another method necessary.

Bazooka Shortcomings

In the Pacific, the various models of the bazooka employed by both the U.S. Army and U.S. Marine Corps proved more than adequate in dealing with the stray Japanese tank. The same could not be said in Europe, between 1944 and 1945, when American soldiers were dealing with heavily armored late war German tanks and self-propelled guns. In this environment, the various models of the bazooka proved a major disappointment, as the bazooka rockets tended to have little or no effect on the enemy armored fighting vehicles, especially on the frontal armor array.

An example of the disappointment felt by American soldiers regarding the performance of their bazookas can be found in a March 1945 U.S. Army report. In that report Corporal Donald E. Lewis mentions his observations on the penetration performance of an American bazooka rocket against that of a German bazooka rocket, both being fired at the same abandoned German Panther tank. Whereas the latter cleanly penetrated the side of and front of the Panther tank, the American bazooka was less successful:

> The American bazooka was fired at the same range. It hit the top of one bogie wheel and failed to penetrate the sides of the tank. The second shot hit the broad side of the tank just above the bogie wheel and left a hole that would barely let light through. It entirely failed to penetrate the front slope.

To overcome the penetration limitation of the American 2.36-inch bazooka, the Ordnance Department began to work on a larger 3.5-inch bazooka firing a more powerful antitank rocket in October 1944. Unfortunately, the fruits of their labor did not appear until after the war was over.

Recoilless Rifles

A late war replacement for the 2.36-inch bazooka was the M18 57mm recoilless rifle. There was also a larger and even more powerful M20 75mm recoilless rifle. Development of the 57mm version had begun in early 1943, and the 75mm version in early 1944. A small number of both weapons reached the field in the last year of the war.

The 57mm recoilless rifle was placed in the heavy weapon squad of infantry companies, while the 75mm recoilless was located in the heavy weapon company of infantry battalions. Both were intended to be employed as direct fire weapons to deal with targets described in a 1948 U.S. Army National Guard manual: '... pillboxes, automatic weapons emplacement, field or artillery gun emplacements, vehicles of all types and grouped personnel.'

The effectiveness of the two recoilless rifles can be seen in this passage from the official multi-volume U.S. Army history of the Second World War titled, *Planning Munitions for War*: 'Reports from users overseas were enthusiastic. Both in the Pacific and in the European theaters, the 57mm and 75mm recoilless rifles proved highly effective against point targets such as tanks and pillboxes.'

Flamethrowers

A weapon that proved very useful in support of American infantry units in the Pacific, but saw a more limited role in Europe, was the individual flamethrower. It had initially been employed by the German Army in 1915 during the First World War and was subsequently adopted by both the French and British armies during the conflict. The U.S. Army had assigned development of an individual flamethrower to the Chemical Warfare Service (CWS) in late 1917. However, the ending of the First World War resulted in the project being canceled, with work on a new flamethrower not being authorized until August 1940.

The first individual flamethrower adopted by the American military was in March 1942. It was designated the M1. The weapon had its combat debut against the Japanese in January 1943, but was not popular because it proved extremely un-reliable. An improved version designated the M1A1 was standardized in late 1942, and began reaching the field in the summer of 1943. It was in turn replaced by a further refined model labeled the M2-2, which initially entered combat in July 1944. In total, 41,452 individual flamethrowers were built for the American military during the Second World War, the majority being the M2-2 model.

Flamethrowers in Combat

Within U.S. Army and U.S. Marine Corps infantry divisions, flamethrowers were assigned to the combat engineer battalion. In the Southwest Pacific some U.S. Army commanders believed that flamethrower men should be made organic members of the infantry rifle squad or platoon, but this never happened. By the close of the Second War, the U.S. Marine Corps had a new divisional TO&E that had the indi-vidual flamethrowers moved from the combat engineer battalion into each infantry regiment.

Found within a U.S. Army report dated May 1, 1945, and titled; *Battle Experiences against the Japanese* is this quote by Lieutenant General R.C. Richardson regarding the use of the weapon and its usefulness:

The infantry places great dependence on flamethrowers. Despite the destructive effects of the naval and air bombardment, many times on Kwajalien it was necessary for the doughboy [a First World War term for American soldiers] to advance under the protection of the flamethrower, throw in phosphorus grenades and then breach the concrete structure with TNT.

From the same report appears this additional extract on the employment of the flamethrower in the Pacific:

An engineer combat battalion had the task of driving Japanese from well-established positions in caves and connecting tunnels … The flamethrower proved the most effective [weapon] because the flame could follow the curves of the cave. The flamethrower was advanced to within effective range under heavy covering fire from rifles and machine guns. After the flamethrower went into action, supporting fire, still maintained, was shifted to enemy individuals as they appeared.

Mortars

During the Second World War the American military employed several types of mortars of various sizes; 60mm, 81mm, and 4.2 inches (107mm). The 60mm mortar was based on a French design, whereas the 81mm and 4.2-inch mortars were based on a British design. In American military service the 60mm mortar was designated the M2, the 81mm the M1, and the 4.2-inch mortar as the 4.2-inch Chemical Mortar. The name, chemical mortar, reflected the fact that the 4.2-inch mortar belonged to the U.S. Army Chemical Warfare Service (CWS) and not the infantry branch of the U.S. Army.

The Ordnance Department issued the first production contracts for the 60mm mortar M2 in early 1940. Production of the 81mm mortar M1 began in late 1939 or early 1940. The 4.2-mortar entered U.S. Army service in the 1920s as a weapon intended only to deliver smoke or poison gas rounds. However, the chief of the CWS saw a need for the weapon to fire high-explosive (HE) rounds, in support of the infantry, and a suitable round was developed in the 1930s, which was approved for service in 1942.

In the American military, the 60mm mortars were located in the weapons platoon of infantry companies, while the 81mm mortar was found in the weapons company of infantry battalions, both being transported by wheeled vehicles. In both rifle companies and rifle battalions, the mortars and the machine guns served as the base of fire for their parent units in both offense and the defense.

In the weapons platoon of U.S. Army infantry rifle companies the 60mm mortars would be located no more than 500 yards behind the company's frontline positions, and it was intended their targets were to be acquired visually. From a Second World War manual is this passage describing the tactical employment of the 81mm mortar:

> The 81mm mortar combines mobility and power in greater degree than any other supporting infantry weapons. Its projectiles have an explosive effect comparable to 75mm projectiles … It is habitually fired from masked positions. When under battalion control, it normally operates in a zone extending 300–800 yards in rear of the leading troops.

Combat Use

The advantages of mortars included great tactical mobility, at least in the case of the American military's 60mm mortar M2 and the 81mm mortar M1, a high rate of fire, a very high trajectory, and adaptability to a variety of terrain conditions. Negative features of mortars included the low muzzle velocity of their finned projectiles and their high trajectory, which meant high winds could reduce their accuracy to unacceptable levels. Another disadvantage of mortars is the difficulty of maintaining a supply of ammunition in combat due to their very high rate of fire.

In a U.S. Army report covering the period between July 1944 and April 1945 in Europe appears this description by the commander of the 22nd Infantry Regiment of how he employed his 60mm mortars:

> I use my 60mm mortars against automatic weapons. When moving against intermittent resistance, one mortar is attached to a rifle platoon. When strong resistance is encountered, the mortars revert to the weapon platoon and are fired from positions 75–100 yards in rear of the leading elements.

From a U.S. Army publication titled *Combat Lessons No. 1* and subtitled *Infantry Weapons in Jungle Warfare*:

> The 81mm mortar proved to be one of the most important single weapons contributing to the success of this offensive. Because of the difficulty of supply only two mortars were taken forward with each heavy-weapons company, the balance of the personnel being used as ammunition carriers. Troops frequently remarked that if given the choice of rations or 81mm mortar ammunition, they would gladly take the latter.

The 4.2-inch Mortar in Combat

Due to its weight and size, the U.S. Army 4.2-inch Chemical Mortar, which served in chemical weapon battalions attached to infantry divisions, served best when the tactical situation was relatively static. The 4.2-inch mortar was originally proposed for a U.S. Marine Corps divisional TO&E of 1940 that was never implemented. It did not appear in any of the succeeding U.S. Marine Corps divisional TO&Es.

The weight and size restrictions of the 4.2-inch mortar were offset by their outstanding efficiency and were emplaced as an infantry support weapon. This shows up in comments made by officers serving in General George S. Patton's Seventh Army during the invasion of Sicily in July 1943. Examples include: '… the equivalent of real artillery.' And '… the most effective single weapon used in support of the infantry.'

A publication titled *Combat Lessons No. 1* contains this passage regarding the employment of the 4.2-inch mortar: 'The 4.2-inch chemical mortar company was placed under the control of the division artillery and the fires of the chemical mortars coordinated with artillery fire.'

An example of the effectiveness of the 4.2-inch mortar that so impressed American soldiers is recounted in this extract from the official U.S. Army multi-volume history of the Second World War:

> Actually, the chemical mortars had the necessary accuracy to engage targets as small as a tracked vehicle. Just before dawn on one of the early days of the Sicily campaign, a temporarily disabled German tank began harassing an infantry position with automatic fire as the crew made repairs. Asked for help by an infantry company, a 2d Chemical Battalion company commander called for one sensing round and then a volley of eight. The tank was silenced. Daylight examination of the tank found all the mortar rounds within an area of 15 yards in diameter, with one of them down the open turret of the vehicle.

Following the Second World War the 4.2-inch Chemical Mortar's proven wartime usefulness resulted in it being made organic to U.S. Army infantry divisions.

Artillery

So badly equipped was the artillery branch of the U.S. Army upon America's entry into the First World War that it had to depend entirely on the acquisition of foreign-supplied artillery pieces to participate in the conflict. This painful embarrassment pushed the U.S. Army to convene a group of artillery officers known as the Westervelt Board, postwar. Their job was to determine what would be needed for the next war and begin their development as quickly as possible.

Funding shortfalls prior to the Second World War prevented large-scale production of the needed artillery pieces recommended by the Westervelt Board, until just before America's official entry into the conflict. The post-First World War artillery pieces that became organic to American infantry divisions during the Second World War included; the 75mm M1A1 Pack Howitzer, the 105mm howitzers M2A1 and M3, and the 155mm howitzer M1.

75mm Howitzer

The first new post-First World War artillery piece to arrive on scene in very small numbers was the 75mm M1 Pack Howitzer, in 1927, later replaced by the M1A1 model. The U.S. Army's chief of field artillery was so pleased with the new howitzer that he stated in a 1932 magazine article: 'It is a remarkable weapon with a great future.' The U.S. Marine Corps adopted the weapon in 1930. When the Japanese attacked Pearl Harbor on 7 December 1941, the U.S. Army had only 458 of the 75mm M1A1 Pack Howitzers in inventory. By the time production of the weapon ended in 1944, a total of 4,939 units had been built.

105mm Howitzers

Work on the development of a new towed 105mm howitzer did not start until the late 1920s. Between 1928 and 1933, fourteen prototypes, designated the M2 were tested. In 1939, the Ordnance Department ordered forty-eight slightly modified units of the M2, designated the M2A1, much against the wishes of the artillery branch of the U.S. Army, which was very much against the weapon, as they felt it was too expensive. They wanted to continue their reliance on an inventory of American-built copies of the famous towed 'French 75' of First World War fame.

It was not until the summer of 1940, when the German military overran France and the Low Countries that the artillery branch of the U.S. Army decided to overlook their objections to the towed 105mm howitzer M2A1 and embrace it. This was due to fact that the American Congress opened its purse to the tune of $9 billion to fund whatever the U.S. Army now desired. It would take three years for the 105mm howitzer M2A1 to replace the last of the obsolete American-built copies of the French 75s. The 105mm howitzer M2A1 would go on to become the workhorse of the American field artillery in the Second World War, with 8,536 units built.

In the field artillery the M2A1 105mm howitzer was classified as a light artillery piece, as appears in this extract from a 5 February, 1944 War Department manual titled *Field Artillery Tactical Employment*:

> Light artillery includes the 105mm howitzer and smaller cannon. Its character-istics are mobility, flexibility of fire, high rate of fire, and rapidity of getting in and out of position. These characteristics, coupled with its range, enable it to render continuous support to other ground forces over areas of great width and depth.

A variant of the 105mm howitzer M2A1 was designated the M3, and like the M2A1, towed into action. It had a shorter barrel than the M2A1 and was mounted on a lighter carriage. It had been ordered by the U.S. Army Ground Forces (AGF) in 1941 to be issued to the new regimental infantry cannon companies that first saw action in North Africa in late 1942 and into early 1943.

Vehicle Mounted 105mm Howitzers

Prior to the towed 105mm howitzer M3 being introduced into U.S. Army service, the regimental cannon companies had been self-propelled, both half-tracked and full-tracked. The half-track version mounting the 105mm howitzer M2A1 was designated the T19, but as indicated by the lack of the letter 'M' in its designation, it was never standardized.

The T19s' full-tracked counterpart in the U.S. Army infantry division was the 105mm Howitzer Motor Carriage (HMC) M7 based on the M3 series of medium tanks. Later production units of the M7 incorporated M4 series medium tank components. The final production version, designated the 105mm HMC M7B1, was based on the chassis of the M4A3 medium tank. Despite the M7 and M7B1 supposedly being intended only for armored divisions, it would remain in some U.S. Army infantry division TO&Es throughout the Second World War. It was adopted at the divisional level by the U.S. Marine Corps in the last year of the war.

155mm Howitzer

In the 1930s, U.S. Army General Lesley J. McNair, a First World War artillery officer, began to suggest that the field artillery had placed too much importance on having large numbers of light artillery pieces (i.e. 75mm) in close support of the infantry. He believed that larger caliber field artillery pieces massing their fire together on important targets would be much more effective on the battlefields of the future. McNair therefore urged that the Army's infantry divisions reduce the number of light howitzers and increase the number of medium howitzers (i.e. 155mm).

McNair's suggestion was not taken up until the German military invasion and quick conquest of France and the Low Countries in the summer of 1940. Upon the French surrender, the U.S. Army adopted a new infantry divisional structure, which included four artillery battalions: three direct support battalions of thirty-six 105mm howitzers and one general support battalion of twelve 155mm howitzers.

The Ordnance Department had begun work on a new 155mm howitzer in 1939, designated the M1, which began reaching the field in 1942. By the end of the Second World War, American factories had built over 6,000 units of the M1 155mm howitzer.

The 155mm howitzer M1 was the replacement for a French-designed 155m howitzer adopted by the U.S. Army during the First World War and eventually designated the 155mm Howitzer, M1918. It was also referred to as the 'Schneider 155mm howitzer'. A total of 2,014 units of the elderly howitzer would be upgraded with a new carriage between 1940 and 1942, with the weapon lasting in American military service in ever decreasing numbers until 1944.

The new M1 155mm howitzer was often referred to by American military artillerymen, be they U.S. Army or U.S. Marine Corps, as 'the sweetest weapon on the front' due to its outstanding accuracy. Within the U.S. Army field artillery the M1 155mm howitzer was classified as a medium artillery piece, as seen in this passage from a 5 February 1944 War Department manual titled; *Field Artillery Tactical Employment*:

> … Medium artillery has a lower rate of fire but greater power than light artillery. Its weight of projectile and range make it preferable to light artillery for counter battery. Its mobility over difficult terrain is appreciably less than that of light artillery.

In the U.S. Marine Corps divisional TO&E of the Second World War, the M1 155mm howitzer was classified as a heavy artillery piece. It had first appeared in the 1st and 2nd Marine Division in 1941 as a replacement for the 105mm howitzers in the divisional TO&E. The other four marine divisions retained the 105mm howitzer until the end of the war, and did not receive any 155mm howitzers until early 1945 as replacements for their 75mm M1A1 Pack Howitzers.

In addition to the M1 155mm Howitzer M1 there was the 4.5-inch Field Gun M1, which fell within the heavy artillery category. It was considered the odd man out, and some have wondered why it was even built. It offered no advantages over the 155mm howitzer M1, and only complicated ammunition supply matters. Despite these factors, 426 units of the 4.5-inch Field Gun M1 were constructed during the Second World, all seeing service in Europe between 1944 and 1945. Externally, it differed from the 155mm howitzer M1 only in having a longer barrel.

U.S. Marine Corps Infantry Support Tanks

The six wartime U.S. Marine Corps infantry divisions were all-arms divisions, meaning that they had organic tank units assigned to them. Prior to and following America's official entry into the Second World War, the U.S. Marine Corps originally preferred light tanks. These included the M2A4 light tank, which saw action at Guadalcanal, but was quickly replaced by the M3 series light tanks, which remained in service until the end of 1943. They were eventually supplemented or replaced by the M5A1 light tank.

Early combat experience showed that the U.S. Marine Corps M3 light tanks lacked the heft to knock down the jungle undergrowth and the firepower needed to deal with Japanese defensive fortifications. Captain Robert L. Denig, Jr. (postwar pro- moted to colonel), who commanded Company B, 2nd Tank Battalion of the U.S. Marine Corps on Guadalcanal, equipped with the M3 [light tank], sums up his feelings on the effectiveness of the vehicle:

> During the Guadalcanal Operation, it became apparent that light tanks, with their 37mm guns and .30 caliber machine guns, were of little value in the jungle, because they were not heavy enough to push their way through the heavy underbrush. In addition, the 37mm gun did not have enough explosive power to destroy machine gun emplacements or concrete bunkers. Because of these

defects, it was decided that medium tanks with 75mm guns would be the main battle tank for the U.S. Marine Corps.

The various versions of the M4 series medium tank employed by the Marines in the Second World War began with the M4A2 model in 1943. It was replaced in most U.S. Marine Corps tank units starting in 1944 by the M4A3 variant. A few M4A1s were also employed by the marines during the Second World War.

U.S. Marine Corps Infantry Support Armored Fighting Vehicles

Adopted by the U.S. Marine Corps during the Second World War was the M3 Gun Motor Carriage (GMC), originally developed by the Ordnance Department as a tank destroyer for the U.S. Army. It was armed with a 75mm gun, the American-built copy of the French 75 from the First World War. Within U.S. Marine Corps divisions, it was found in the regimental antitank platoons and division antitank companies.

Due to the small number of Japanese tanks encountered by the Marines in the Pacific, the M3 GMC was primarily employed as an assault gun to deal with enemy defensive works. The vehicle would last in service with the marines until early 1945.

Another U.S. Army armored fighting vehicle adopted by the U.S. Marine Corps was the M3A1 Scout Car, an open-topped four-wheel drive vehicle armed with a number of machine guns. American industry built approximately 21,000 units of the M3A1 Scout Car between 1939 and 1944. In early 1942, the Marines took on a number of them, but soon decided that the quarter-ton Jeep was a much more practical vehicle and quickly discarded the M3A1s it had acquired.

A much more useful series of vehicles that served with the U.S. Army and the U.S. Marine Corps in the Pacific, and in Europe with the U.S. Army in relatively small numbers, was referred to as the Landing Vehicle Tracked (LVT). It was an amphibious tractor that came in both armored and non-armored variants. Originally intended strictly as a cargo transport vehicle it was soon pressed into a makeshift machine gun armed and armored amphibious personnel carrier by the U.S. Marine Corps. As time went on, more specialized versions appeared as gun/howitzer armed fire-support vehicles.

The LVT series, LVT-1 through LVT-3, was organic to the U.S. Marine Corps divisional TO&E in 1942 and 1943. Most became non-divisional assets in 1944. Some were retained by the divisional non-infantry units, such as the engineers. The LVTs were never organic to the TO&E of U.S. Army infantry divisions.

U.S. Marine Corps Infantry Support Antiaircraft Guns

Organic to the U.S. Marine Corps infantry divisions in 1942, but not to U.S. Army infantry divisions, were several antiaircraft guns of various calibers. These included a land-based 20mm antiaircraft gun in both single and twin mounts. There was also the

40mm Automatic Gun M1, and the 90mm Gun M1, as well as the improved version designated the M1A1.

The 20mm and 40mm antiaircraft guns were foreign-designed weapons license-built in American factories. The 40mm was popularly referred to as the 'Bofors', which was the name of the Swedish firm that had designed it. The 90mm antiaircraft gun was an American-designed and built weapon. The 20mm and 40mm antiaircraft guns were standard shipboard weapons for the U.S. Navy for most of the Second World War.

As the war progressed and lessons were learned, the U.S. Marine Corps made a number of changes to their divisional TO&E. These included the removal of the 20mm and 90mm antiaircraft guns from the divisional level in 1943. The 40mm anti-aircraft guns lasted at the divisional level until 1944. The disappearance of the last of the divisional antiaircraft assets late in the war reflected the complete American military air superiority attained at that time.

In this interwar period photograph, taken during a U.S. Army training exercise, is a Mark I 3-inch Stokes mortar and crew on the right, and the crew of an M1916 37mm Gun on the left. The mortar was British-designed and the 37mm gun was French-designed. Both were produced under license in the United States during the First World War and employed postwar. (NA)

(*Opposite above*) Being pulled by hand in this pre-Second World War photograph is an M1916 37mm Gun during a U.S. Army training maneuver. Typically, during the First World War, the weapon would be removed from its wheeled carriage prior to firing. Aiming in the direct-fire mode was accomplished with a telescopic sight. It could also be fired in indirect fire mode. (*NA*)

(*Above*) With some shrubbery employed as camouflage, the U.S. Army crew of a 37mm Gun M3A1, mounted on a two-wheel towed carriage designated the M4A1, guard a crossroads during a training exercise sometime before America's official entry into the Second World War. The weapon had a rate of fire of 15–20 rounds per minute. (*NA*)

(*Opposite below*) The crew of a U.S. Marine Corps 37mm Gun M3A1 is shown emplaced in action. The weapon had a high-explosive round with a maximum range of 12,800 yards. For close-range protection, the gun was supplied with an anti-personnel canister round that proved very effective. The 950lb weapon could be traversed 60 degrees from its centerline, elevated 15 degrees and depressed minus 10 degrees. (*NA*)

(*Opposite above*) The 37mm Gun M3A1 seen here also fired a 0.53lb armor-piercing round, which had a muzzle velocity of 2,900 feet per second. In theory, the armor-piercing round was supposed to be able to penetrate 2.4 inches of steel armor at a range of 500 yards. The battlefield reality demonstrated in North Africa showed the weapon armor-piercing round was useless against the frontal armor array of German medium tanks. (*NA*)

(*Opposite below*) The replacement for the 37mm Gun M3A1 proved to be 57mm Gun M1, which is seen here, and could be mounted on a number of slightly different two wheeled towed carriages, the most common being the M1A3. In the 1943 TO&E of a U.S. Army infantry division there were a total of fifty-four units of the 57mm Gun M1, with eighteen in each of the division's three infantry regiments. (*NA*)

(*Above*) The carriage for the 57mm Gun M1 provided it with 45 degrees of right and left traverse. It could be elevated 15 degrees and depressed minus 5 degrees. The gun and carriage together weighed 2,810lbs. Firing a 2.25lb armor-piercing projectile at 2,800 feet per second, it was supposed to be able to penetrate almost 4 inches of steel armor at 1,000 yards. (*NA*)

(*Above*) The gun shield on the 57mm Gun M1 was proof only against bullet fragments. A U.S. Army report noted that the weapon's gun shield's psychological value was of more importance than its actual protective ability. According to a 1942 U.S. Army manual it was recommended that the gun crew not open fire at enemy tanks at ranges greater than 800 yards. (*NA*)

(*Opposite above*) A line of U.S. Army soldiers have formed a human chain to funnel ammunition to a 57mm Gun M1. With a well-practised crew, the 57mm Gun M1 had a rate of fire of 12–15 rounds per minute. Initially there was only an armor-piercing round available for the gun when it was fielded in 1943. It took until late 1944 before an American-made high-explosive round became available for the weapon. (*NA*)

(*Opposite below*) A 57mm Gun M1 is being unlimbered by its crew from an M2A1 armored half-track. The weight of the weapon made it extremely difficult to move and emplace once detached from its towing vehicle. Even when emplaced in a defensive position, it was very vulnerable to enemy fire, as it was often located in close proximity to the main line of resistance established by an infantry battalion or regiment. (*NA*)

Pictured is the crew of a U.S. Army M1A1 2.36-inch Antitank Rocket Launcher (best known as the Bazooka) prepared to fire their weapon. The circular see-through plastic item located at the end of the barrel was referred to as a flash deflector. The Bazooka barrel was 54 inches long and weighed 13.25lbs when empty. It had front and rear sights mounted on the left side of the barrel. (NA)

Two U.S. Army infantrymen pose with an M1A1 2.36-inch Bazooka and the M6A1 antitank rocket it fired. The soldier holding the bazooka is gripping (with his left hand) the front wooden hand grip, which included the trigger and trigger guard. The wedge-shaped wooden stock behind the front hand grip was shaped to fit against the firer's shoulder. It also contained the batteries that ignited the rocket when the trigger was pulled. (NA)

The wartime M1A1 2.36-inch Bazooka team consisted of two men as seen here: the loader, who is shown inserting an M6A1 antitank rocket into the rear of the weapon's barrel, and the firer. The maximum range of the rocket was 700 yards. However, the effective range of the rocket was 300 yards or less when engaging enemy tanks or armored fighting vehicles. (NA)

An American soldier is shown firing his M1A1 2.36-inch Bazooka at the enemy from the cover of an earthen embankment. When the propellant in the M6A1 rocket motor was ignited in the launcher tube, gases and flames were blown from the rear of the device. This back blast required the area behind the launcher to be clear of both personnel and flammable material in a radius of 25 yards. (NA)

An American soldier holds an M1A1 2.36-inch Bazooka in his left hand and a captured German version designated the 8.8cm *Raketen Panzerbuchse* 54, also known as the *Panzerschreck* (Tank Terror), in his right hand. The German weapon was a larger and more powerful reverse-engineered version of the American Bazooka first issued in 1943. (NA)

The U.S. Army soldier in the background is armed with the original M1A1 2.36-inch Bazooka, while the soldier in the foreground is armed with its improved replacement, referred to as M9A1. Unlike the M1A1 2.36-inch Bazooka the new M9A1 2.36-inch Bazooka could be folded in half for ease of storage. The wooden shoulder stock seen on the M1A1 was replaced with a metal shoulder rest on the M9A1. (NA)

A new weapon adopted by the American military during the last year of the Second World War was the M18 57mm recoilless rifle seen here perched on the shoulder of a U.S. Army soldier. The 45lb weapon had an approximate length of five feet and could also be fired from a tripod if need be. As with the Bazookas it replaced, the M18 57mm recoilless rifle was serviced by a crew of two men. (NA)

(*Opposite above*) The M18 57mm recoilless rifle shown here on the shoulder of a U.S. Army soldier was the replacement for the M1A1 and M9A1 Bazookas. Besides packing more penetrative punch than its predecessors, it also offered an increase in range. In the early postwar era, it was replaced in American military service by the M20 3.5-inch rocket launcher. (*NA*)

(*Opposite below*) The larger cousin of the M18 57mm recoilless rifle fielded during the last year of the war with the American military was the M20 recoilless rifle. Due to its weight of 114.5lb, the almost seven foot long weapon could only be fired from a tripod, as seen in this picture. (*NA*)

(*Above*) A U.S. Army officer in Europe is shown holding a disconnected M2 flame gun. The rear hand grip had a lever allowing the operator of the flamethrower to control the flow of the fuel and the amount of flame being produced. Visible on the crate behind the officer is an upright M2-2 flamethrower, which would be employed with the M2 flame gun. (*NA*)

A marine points out a potential target for another marine armed with the M2-2 flamethrower. Empty, the weapon weighed 43lbs; with a full load of fuel it weighed 68–72lbs. Not only did the actual flame of the weapon cause casualties among enemy personnel, but the sight of the flame and smoke produced by the weapon would sometime cause enemy troops to abandon their defensive positions. (NA)

Here we see two marines armed with the M2-2 flamethrower firing upon an enemy defensive position. When employed against enemy defensive works flamethrowers were extremely useful, as they could explode ammunition and any explosives stored within them. The flamethrowers also had the ability to shoot around corners, as the blazing thickened fuel would ricochet from wall to wall within enemy fortifications. (NA)

A marine with an M2-2 flamethrower takes a break from the fighting to light a cigarette. The fuel used in the flame-throwers consisted of one can of thickened napalm weighing 5¼ lbs with 20 gallons of gasoline. Thickened fuel was preferred, as it offered twice the range of liquid fuel. The other advantage of thickened fuel is that most of it clings to and burns, in or on a target, for as long as six minutes. (NA)

(*Above*) The U.S. Army soldier in the background has his right hand on the traversing hand wheel of a 60mm Mortar M2, and was referred to as the 'gunner'. The soldier in the foreground was referred to as the 'No. 2 man', and was tasked with loading the weapon. When the shell was dropped, both the gunner and number two-man would duck their heads to protect their faces from the muzzle blast. (*NA*)

(*Opposite above*) The 60mm Mortar M2 seen here with its U.S. Army crew weighed 42lbs with bipod and mount fitted. The normal rate of fire of the weapon was around 18 rounds per minute, with the maximum rate of fire listed as 30–35 rounds per minute. Firing its standard high-explosive round, it had a maximum range of up to 1,985 yards. (*NA*)

(*Opposite below*) Pictured is the two-man U.S. Marine Corps crew of a 60mm Mortar M2. An interesting comment, regarding the use of the weapon when confronted by heavy undergrowth, came out in a May 1945 report: 'Because jungle vegetation limits the effective radius of bursts, mortar concentrations can be placed very close to our own lines. Often 60mm mortars were adjusted to within 25 or 35 yards of our own troops.' (*NA*)

(*Opposite above*) The U.S. Army soldier in the right foreground is conversing on his SCR 536 radio, and no doubt relating firing coordinates to the gunner for the 60mm Mortar M2 pictured, which is being loaded with a shell. The standard high-explosive shell for the weapon was labeled the M49A2 and was a fragmentation shell that would break into over 200 fragments when it exploded. (*NA*)

(*Opposite below*) The U.S. Army crew of an 81mm Mortar M1 is shown cleaning the barrel after a firing mission. Including the barrel, bipod, and base plate, the weapon weighed 130lbs. Like the smaller 60mm Mortar M2, the typical rate of fire was 18 rounds per minute, with a maximum rate of fire of 30–35 rounds. The maximum range of the weapon was approximately 3,290 yards. (*NA*)

(*Above*) The U.S. Army crew of this 81mm Mortar M1 have dug a rather deep emplacement for protection from enemy artillery or mortars. For aiming the weapon there was a collimator optical sight on the left-hand side of the barrel designated the M4. It was combined with a direct sight. The weapon was capable of firing an effective concentration in an area of 100 × 100 yards. (*NA*)

(*Above*) Based on the amount of stored ammunition in this picture the crew of this U.S. Army 81mm Mortar M1 are anticipating that they will be very busy. A number of different rounds were fired by the weapon. The Shell, High-Explosive, M43A1 was intended for use against enemy personnel, while the larger Shell, High-Explosive, M56 was used against light enemy defensive works. (*NA*)

(*Opposite page*) A U.S. Army mortar man receives aiming coordinates for his 81mm Mortar M1 over a landline. There was a smoke round designated the Shell, Chemical, M57 for the weapon. From a wartime U.S. Army report comes this extract on the employment of the 81mm smoke shell: 'When we fire a preparation with mortars the last round from each weapon is smoke. When the infantry see the smoke they advance ...' (*NA*)

(*Above*) Seldom photographed during the war but of key importance for the fast-firing 81mm Mortar M1 were the men seen here who carried the weapon's ammunition from the supply point to the weapon's firing position. Through experimentation, it was discovered that Japanese 81mm mortar ammunition could be fired from its American counterpart and was therefore used on occasion. (*NA*)

(*Opposite page*) Marines are shown preparing to fire their 81mm Mortar M1, with one man appearing to be checking a range chart. From a report regarding the fighting in the Pacific appears this extract: 'As many mortars as possible must be placed to reach any area in front of the main line of resistance to a depth of 300 yards. By doing so, enemy attacks frequently can be broken as they deploy.' (*NA*)

(*Above*) Pictured are two heavily braced 4.2-inch chemical mortars in action. The German Army general in charge of their chemical warfare branch stated after the war that 'from the technical point of view the American 4.2" chemical projector is very good; the construction is simple, it is a very handy weapon in battle and its firing efficiency is high.' (*NA*)

(*Opposite above*) Often attached to U.S. Army infantry divisions was the 4.2-inch Chemical Mortar seen in this picture. The high-explosive shell for the weapon weighed 32lbs. It had a maximum range of 4,400 yards. Notice the sandbags arrayed around the bottom of the weapon to help steady it when firing due to the heavy recoil it generated. (*NA*)

(*Opposite below*) A 4.2-inch chemical mortar battery is shown in action. The weapon, with all its various components, weighed 333lbs. It could be broken down into three pieces for ease of transport, but each piece still weighed too much for an individual soldier to carry. It was therefore typically brought into firing position by a wheeled vehicle, or in very rough terrain, by mules. (*NA*)

(*Opposite above*) On display at the now closed U.S. Army Ordnance Museum is this 75mm Gun, M1897. It is mounted to the Carriage M2A2 optimized for high speed towing. The gun was a pre-First World War design adopted by the U.S. Army during the First World War. The modernized licence-built copies of the weapon remained in U.S. Army inventory as an artillery field piece and antitank gun up until the very early stages of the Second World War. (*NA*)

(*Opposite below*) Pictured in this pre-Second World War photo is a U.S. Army 75mm Howitzer M1A1 on an M3A1 split trail carriage. The Ordnance Department assigned two separate designations to its towed antitank guns and artillery pieces. The first was for the weapon itself and the second for the wheeled carriage it was mounted on. (*NA*)

(*Above*) Marines man a 75mm Howitzer M1A1 on an M1 box carriage. The howitzer weighed 341lbs and could fire up to 6 rounds per minute. Its 75mm high-explosive rounds, which weighed 17.32–18.12lbs, had a maximum range of 9,700 yards. For ease of transport, the M1 box carriage could be broken down into six loads. (*NA*)

(*Above*) The light weight of the 75mm Howitzer M1A1, relative to larger artillery pieces, and its ability to be broken down into pieces, meant it was popular with the U.S. Marine Corps in some of its island campaigns, because it could be disassembled and then reassembled in areas that were inaccessible to larger artillery pieces. Here we see a marine-manned 75mm Howitzer M1A1 engaging an enemy bunker on a mountainside. (*NA*)

(*Opposite above*) U.S. Army soldiers are shown manning a 75mm Howitzer M1A1. During the Second World War the U.S. Army's inventory of the weapon was concentrated in its three airborne divisions and a single mountain division. In a February 1944 TO&E the airborne divisions were authorized thirty-six units of 75mm Howitzer M1A1. This rose to sixty units of the weapon in revised TO&E December 1944. (*NA*)

(*Opposite below*) An early model 105mm Howitzer M2A1 is shown on display. There were thirty-six 105mm howitzers assigned to Second World War American infantry divisions. They were divided between three artillery battalions, each further sub-divided into three batteries of four howitzers each. In combat, a single 105mm field artillery battalion would typically be tasked with supporting one of the three infantry regiments that made up an infantry division. (*NA*)

(*Above*) Here we see a U.S. Marine Corps 105mm Howitzer M2A1 in use with the gun barrel in recoil. The weapon's rate of fire was between 2 and 4 rounds per minute. The types of fire missions assigned to the 105mm howitzer and the effect sought were defined as neutralization, destruction, registration, harassing, or interdiction. (*NA*)

(*Opposite above*) Pictured is a 105mm Howitzer M2A1 being fired at maximum elevation of 64 degrees. Mounted on the M2A3 carriage, the weapon weighed 4,980lbs, and was typically towed into action by a wheeled vehicle. The maximum range of the 105mm howitzer was approximately 12,000 yards. The standard round was high-explosive and weighed 33lbs. (*NA*)

(*Opposite below*) A 'cannoneer' is shown loading a 105mm Howitzer M2A1. From a U.S. Army report done on the fighting in North Africa in 1943 appears this comment: 'The 105mm howitzer, with indirect fire, is not effective against single tanks. Precision fire against moving tanks is impossible. Hold your fire until the tanks bunch, and then mass the fire of a battalion on them …' (*NA*)

U.S. Army artillerymen are shown setting the fuze on a high-explosive round for a 105mm Howitzer M2A1. The most common fire mission for the 105mm howitzer was neutralization. It was defined in manuals as 'Fire delivered on areas to destroy the combat efficiency of enemy personnel by causing severe losses and interrupting movement of action ...' (NA)

Pictured in use is a U.S. Army 105mm Howitzer M3. The weapon was a lightweight version of the M2A1 105mm Howitzer, with a shortened barrel, originally intended for use by the U.S. Army's airborne divisions. They saw more widespread employment in the cannon companies of infantry regiments, with each regimental cannon company having six of the 105mm Howitzer M3. (NA)

The primary mission of the 105mm Howitzer M3 (an example is shown here), in regimental cannon companies according to wartime manuals was the following: '... to destroy or neutralize hostile troops and weapons which at the time offer the greatest threat to the accomplishment of the regimental mission, and which cannot be engaged as readily by the support artillery' (i.e. divisional artillery battalions). (NA)

(*Opposite above*) The smoke emanating from the barrel of the 105mm Howitzer M3 pictured indicates it had just been fired. According to the wartime manual on the weapon, it was optimized to destroy enemy automatic weapons, antitank guns, roadblocks, pillboxes, and strongly fortified buildings. It was not to take the place of the infantry division's four artillery battalions, but supplement them on the battlefield. (*NA*)

(*Opposite below*) Pictured is a 75mm Howitzer Motor Carriage (HMC) T30, which had a five-man crew. The White Motor Company began series production of the 10.25-ton vehicle in February 1942. Production continued through November 1943, with a total of 500 units completed. The other version mounting the 105mm howitzer was designated the T19 HMC. (*NA*)

(*Above*) Prior to the introduction of the towed 105mm Howitzer M3 into infantry regimental cannon companies, the U.S. Army equipped those infantry divisions fighting in North Africa, and later in Sicily, with M3 series armored half-tracks mounting either the 75mm Howitzer M1A1, or in the case of the vehicle pictured, the 105mm M2A1. (*NA*)

(*Opposite above*) The eventual replacement for the T30 and T19 within some regimental cannon companies that fought in Sicily in 1943 was the full-tracked M7 105mm Howitzer Motor Carriage (HMG) seen here, until the 105mm Howitzer M3 became available. The M7 and the M7A1 were typically found in the field artillery battalions of armored divisions. (*NA*)

(*Opposite below*) Seen here in North Africa in 1943 is a U.S. Army 155mm Howitzer, M1918. It is mounted on the carriage designated the M1918A3, which featured pneumatic wheels so it could be towed behind high speed wheeled vehicles. The First World War era 155mm howitzer piece was supposed to have been replaced in service before the Second World War, but budget shortfalls kept it in service during the conflict. (*NA*)

(*Above*) Pictured having just been fired is a U.S. Marine Corps 155mm Howitzer M1, the replacement for the 155mm Howitzer, M1918 in American military service. Each U.S. Army infantry division, and later U.S. Marine Corps infantry division, had a single battalion of twelve of these weapons divided between three batteries, each with four 155mm howitzers. (*NA*)

(*Above*) Seen here in full recoil is a U.S. Army 155mm Howitzer M1. The weapon on its carriage weighed 3,825lbs and was towed into action by a wheeled vehicle. Due to the size and weight of its ammunition, approximately 108lbs, the 155mm Howitzer M1 had a rate of fire of only 2 rounds per minute. (*NA*)

(*Opposite above*) The 155mm Howitzer M1 shown here was classified as a medium artillery piece by the U.S. Army, while the U.S. Marine Corps considered it a heavy artillery piece. The maximum range of the weapon was 16,000 yards. It was most often employed for the sole purpose of destroying material objects, in contrast to the 105mm howitzer, which was used to destroy personnel. (*NA*)

(*Opposite below*) Pictured is an M2A4 light tank coming off a landing craft. It was used briefly by the U.S. Marine Corps in the early part of the fighting in the Pacific until replaced by a more modern light tank. The M2A4 main gun was designated the 37mm gun M5, which was a shortened version of the infantry's towed 37mm Gun M3A1. (*NA*)

The replacement for the M2A4 light tank in U.S. Marine Corps service was the M3 light tank seen here. It was not a new vehicle but a progressive update of the M2A4 light tank. Early-production units went into battle with the same 37mm gun M5 as mounted in the M2A4. Late-production units of the M3 were armed with an improved version of the 37mm gun referred to as the M6. (NA)

Obviously somebody told the U.S. Marine Corps crew to look busy for the guy who took this picture of a mid-production light tank M3 with a welded-armor turret and riveted hull. The light tank M3 retained both the vehicle commander's cupola and sponson-mounted .30 caliber machine guns from the light tank M2A4. (NA)

The eventual light tank replacement for the M3 in the U.S. Marine Corps was the progressively updated M5A1 light tank, with two visible in this picture, the leading tank in the column and the tank bringing up the rear of the three tank column. The key identifying design features of the M5A1 were the sloping upper front hull plate and the elongated turret. (NA)

Early combat experience showed the U.S. Marine Corps that its light tanks lacked the heft to push through jungle undergrowth and the firepower to deal with Japanese defensive works. The U.S. Marine Corps therefore sought out the gasoline-engine powered M4 or M4A1 medium tanks from U.S. Army stockpiles. What they got instead was the diesel-engine powered M4A2 medium tank seen here. (NA)

(*Above*) Here we see a U.S. Marine Corps M4A2 medium tank with a captured Japanese light tank positioned on its rear engine deck. One can assume that it will be transported to a rear area as a war trophy. Unhappy at first with the diesel-powered M4A2 medium tanks, the Marine tankers quickly began to appreciate the fact that their diesel-powered tanks were far less susceptible to fire than those powered by gasoline engines. (*NA*)

(*Opposite above*) With very little threat from Japanese tanks in the Pacific, the M4A2 medium tanks issued to the U.S. Marine Corps concentrated on infantry support missions, as seen in this picture, with marines crouching behind the tank for cover from enemy fire. Visible on the side of the tank hull is wooden planking intended to minimize the threat from Japanese hand-held magnetic mines. (*NA*)

(*Opposite below*) When the U.S. Marine Corps exhausted its inventory of diesel-powered M4A2 medium tanks they returned to the U.S. Army for additional M4 series medium tanks. What they got was the gasoline engine powered, second-generation, M4A3 medium tank, a disabled example seen here stuck in a ditch. Reflecting the dire threat posed by suicidal Japanese infantry antitank teams, the tank's hatches are covered with nails point up, and the engine deck with sandbags. (*NA*)

(*Opposite above*) This second-generation M4A3 medium tank in U.S. Marine Corps service has in lieu of wooden planking on the side of its hull, extra track links welded on not only the side of the hull, but also the turret and front hull. To increase the level of cooperation between tanks and infantry in combat, field telephones were placed at the rear of the vehicles. (*NA*)

(*Opposite below*) To deal with Japanese defensive positions, the U.S. Marine Corps first employed light tanks armed with flamethrowers. The results were disappointing and the decision was made to employ the M4 series tank as a flamethrower platform. The M4 series tanks were modified to accommodate turret-mounted flame guns, in place of the 75mm main gun, and were designated as the PAO-CWS-H1, one of which is seen in action in this image. (*NA*)

(*Above*) Pictured is a U.S. Army PAO-CWS-H1 in action in the Pacific. The troops nicknamed them 'Zippos', the brand name of a popular cigarette lighter renowned for its reliability. The first batch of POA-CWS-H1 tanks consisted of eight U.S. Army M4A3 medium tanks. All eight would see action during the conquest of Iwo Jima between February and March 1945, in support of marines. (*NA*)

(*Above*) Many felt that the POA-CWS-H1 would be better off if the 75mm main gun could be retained for self-protection. In response, the marines ordered seventy-two units of a new version of the tank that had both a flame gun and the standard 75mm main gun as seen here in this museum display vehicle. The new model flamethrower tank was designated the POA-CWS-H5, but arrived too late to see combat. (*Loren Hannah*)

(*Opposite above*) Another U.S. Army vehicle adopted by the U.S. Marine Corps during the Second World War was the 75mm Gun Motor Carriage (GMC) M3/M3A1, seen here coming off a landing ship tank (LST) in the Pacific. It was armed with the 75mm Gun, M1897, and was originally intended by the U.S. Army to be a tank destroyer. The marines took it into service as an assault gun. (*NA*)

(*Opposite below*) A number of marines are shown hitching a ride on a 75mm Gun Motor Carriage (GMC) M3. The maximum armor thickness on the vehicle was 0.625 inches (15.9mm) on the gun shield. The gun could be traversed 19 degrees left, and 21 degrees right on the M3 model. On the later M3A1 version, the gun could be traversed 21 degrees left or right. (*NA*)

(*Above*) An armored vehicle that was employed by the U.S. Marine Corps was the M3A1 Scout Car seen here. The example pictured shows pre-Second World War U.S. Army markings. The 10,000lb open-topped vehicle had a crew of three and was armed with three machine guns. It was issued to marine scout companies and other units briefly in 1942, but was soon replaced by the lighter and more useful Jeep. (*Michael Green*)

(*Opposite above*) Until the Marine Corps invasion of the island of Betio in the Tarawa Atoll, which took place in November 1943, the LVT-1 seen here had been used by the U.S. Marine Corps strictly as a supply vehicle in unopposed landings. In preparation for the assault on the well-defended island of Betio, improvised armor was added to the LVT-1. (*NA*)

(*Opposite below*) The LVT-1 had a number of design problems centered mainly on its fragile suspension system, which proved too vulnerable to the corrosive effects of saltwater, and as a result had a very short lifespan. To resolve this issue, a new, much improved amphibious tracked vehicle, designated the LVT-2 was placed into service. An armored version is seen here. (*NA*)

(*Above*) The LVT(A)1 shown here was no longer just a cargo carrier but an amphibious tank based on the chassis of the LVT(A)2. A superstructure extending from the front crew cab over the vehicle's centrally mounted cargo compartment was topped off by a 37mm main gun-armed turret, seen here, with 360 degrees of traverse. (*NA*)

(*Opposite above*) Combat experience showed the LVT(A)1 to be both under-armored and under-gunned. Adding additional armor to the vehicle and the resulting weight penalty would have impacted the sea-handling characteristics of the LVT(A)1, so that option was discarded. However, it did prove possible to up-gun the vehicle with a 75mm howitzer, as seen here, resulting in the designation LVT(A)4. (*NA*)

(*Opposite below*) The last amphibious tracked vehicle to enter into U.S. Marine Corps service during the Second World War was the LVT-3. An improved, postwar version designated the LVT-3C is seen here on display at the Marine Corps Landing Vehicle Tracked Museum, located at Camp Pendleton in Southern California. The vehicle was 24 feet 6 inches long, 11 feet 2 inches wide, and 9 feet 11 inches high. (*Michael Green*)

(*Above*) Marines man a 40mm Automatic Gun M1. The weight of the gun and carriage was 5,549lbs. Rate of fire was 120 rounds per minute, with the weapon's maximum vertical range being 7,625 yards. The projectile portion of the 4.82lb round weighed 2.06lbs and had a muzzle velocity of 2,870 feet per second. (*NA*)

(*Opposite above*) A marine prepares to load a high-explosive round into the breach of a 90mm Antiaircraft Gun M1. The weapon with its carriage weighed 19,000lbs and was designed to be able to engage high-flying bombers. The rate of fire with the 42lb round was 25 per minute. The maximum effective ceiling of the 90mm antiaircraft gun was approximately 34,000 feet. (*NA*)

A U.S. Marine Corps 90mm Antiaircraft M1 is shown being operated by African-American marines. The U.S. Marine Corps was not averse to using it for other roles, as seen in this extract from a wartime report: 'Four 90mm antiaircraft guns were sited along the crest of a ridge on the perimeter and used in direct fire against Jap gun positions and small groups of Japs. Results were excellent. It is believed these guns destroyed five enemy 75mm guns.' (NA)